Editor
Eric Migliaccio
Jennifer Overend Prior, M. Ed.

Managing Editor
Ina Massler Levin, M.A.

Editor-in-Chief
Sharon Coan, M.S. Ed.

Illustrator
Reneé Christine Yates

Cover Artist
Barb Lorseyedi

Art Coordinator
Kevin Barnes

Imaging
Rosa C. See

Product Manager
Phil Garcia

Publishers
Rachelle Cracchiolo, M.S. Ed.
Mary Dupuy Smith, M.S. Ed.

Early Childhood Literacy Centers

W9-BZH-653

Author

Traci Ferguson Geiser, M.A.

Teacher Created Materials, Inc.
6421 Industry Way
Westminster, CA 92683
www.teachercreated.com
ISBN-0-7439-3717-1
Reprinted, 2003
©2003 Teacher Created Materials, Inc.
Made in U.S.A.

Table of Contents

Table of Contents *(cont.)*

Introduction

The Early Childhood Centers series was created especially for busy teachers of young children. The hands-on, developmentally appropriate activities are sure to provide your students with hours of fun-filled learning experiences throughout the year. The activities are set up in an easy-to-follow format and require little preparation time and few materials. Each center is designed to reinforce skills typically taught in early childhood programs. The Skills Reference Chart on pages 8 and 9 will guide you as you blend the activities with your existing curriculum.

Early Childhood Literacy Centers provides young children with opportunities to practice skills that will prepare them for reading and writing. Each chapter offers several different activities to reinforce literacy skills. The centers in each chapter vary in level of difficulty and provide for different learning styles in order to meet the individual needs of each of your students.

The chapters will focus on the following skills:

- **Alphabet Sequencing:** These activities are designed to help children become familiar with the alphabet and the sequence of the letters. The centers begin very simply with part of the alphabet and later include whole alphabet activities. The first few centers focus on uppercase letters only for the youngest learners, as they can be easier to recognize than their lowercase counterparts. If your program introduces both uppercase and lowercase letters simultaneously, you may want to write in the lowercase letters on these activities. The whole alphabet activities include both lowercase and uppercase letters for children who have mastered the uppercase alphabet.

- **Uppercase and Lowercase Letters:** Each center in this chapter will help students recognize and match uppercase letters to their lowercase counterparts. These activities are best suited for children who have mastered the more easily recognizable uppercase letters and are ready to begin working with lowercase letters. Partial alphabet activities are presented before the entire alphabet is used.

- **Initial Consonants:** Once your students are feeling comfortable with the letters of the alphabet, you can begin to help them learn the sounds that each letter makes. These centers will give children ample practice matching easy-to-recognize pictures with their initial consonants. You may wish to use the partial alphabet activities before working with the full alphabet activities.

Introduction *(cont.)*

- **Rhyming Words and Word Families:** Developing an understanding of rhyming words is an important prereading skill. Building an oral language base helps children as they begin to read. Working with the sounds of words and identifying rhyming words are vital first steps in literacy development. Centers in this chapter will give your students fun, hands-on opportunities to practice with rhyming words and word families.

- **Fine Motor Skills:** Building fine motor control is essential for beginning writers. These fun centers will provide your class with practice in writing, cutting, and strengthening the many muscles in the hands and fingers.

- **Visual Discrimination:** Little eyes need practice discriminating letters, shapes and designs that are similar. This important skill will help children differentiate letters and words as they begin to read. Centers in this chapter will give children several opportunities to discriminate between similar, yet different, symbols and letters.

- **Long and Short Vowels:** As children begin to learn vowel sounds, these activities will provide practice with hearing the sound that each long and short vowel makes. Discrimination between long and short vowel sounds is also a focus of these centers.

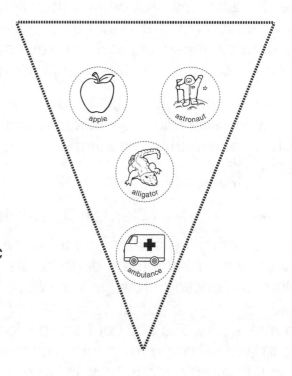

- **Basic Sight Words:** Children will encounter high-frequency words as they begin to read. Color words, number words, shape words and a few other basic sight words are found in many beginning reading texts. Giving children an opportunity to begin recognizing sight words through these center activities will give them a jump-start as they begin to read.

- **Mini Books:** Adults feel more comfortable trying something new if they have been given some information or the opportunity to practice before they try it. Children, too, will feel much more comfortable as they begin to read if they have had opportunities to practice and gather information about books. The mini books centers focus on various aspects of books while reinforcing literacy skills. Children and parents will delight in the experience of reading these books together.

Introduction *(cont.)*

What Is a Center Activity?

A center activity is designed to give children individual or small group practice in developing skills. The activities are usually easy for children to accomplish with little or no assistance from the teacher. While students work on independent center activities, the teacher is free to work with a child or small group of children without interruption.

The *Early Childhood Centers* series was designed with young learners in mind. Each book in the series features developmentally appropriate, hands-on activities to engage and hold the attention of young children.

Why Use Centers?

Center activities provide opportunities for children to learn how to work independently while learning essential skills. Most centers feature methods for student self-checking that enables children to check their work and, if necessary, problem solve to find the correct answer.

Children working in small groups during center time can teach each other valuable skills and information through their work together. Group problem solving can lead to meaningful discoveries that can have a lasting effect on learning.

Center Assembly and Organization

At the beginning of each center activity, a Teacher Preparation section informs you of what needs to be done before the center is presented to the class. The Materials section provides you with a list of all the materials the children will need in order to complete the center. Unless otherwise specified, you will need to make only one copy of each designated reproducible. You may also choose to color and laminate the centers for visual appeal and durability. Puzzle pieces should be cut out carefully, making sure to cut around the tab pieces. If you wish to use the puzzles simply for matching you may cut the tabs off.

Prior to center time, it is important to thoroughly explain each center so every child has a clear understanding of what he or she is expected to do. The Student Directions section of each center gives clear step-by-step instructions for completing the center activity. The first day of a center rotation will require a little extra time to explain each center. On subsequent days, children who have completed a center can help describe the center activity to their classmates.

Introduction *(cont.)*

Always include a discussion of where and how the center materials are to be cleaned up and stored. Envelopes and plastic baggies are wonderful organizational materials. Label each envelope or baggie and the accompanying game pieces with matching stickers to indicate where each set of game pieces are to be stored. This will help keep materials organized and enable children to clean up materials easily. Small shoeboxes or trays may be helpful for storing center materials when they are not in use.

How Do I Manage Centers?

Center activities are best used when they are a part of the daily routine. A twenty- to thirty-minute block of the day is ample time for conducting learning centers. During this time, children may be put in small groups by the teacher and assigned names (red group, blue group etc.). The groups may rotate each day until each group has had the opportunity to complete each center. A simple color chart with clothespins (see the illustration below) helps manage this rotation.

If you prefer a less structured use of centers, you may wish to allow your students to choose the centers where they would like to work. In this case, you may want to limit the number of children in each center to be sure you have adequate supplies for each child to complete his or her task.

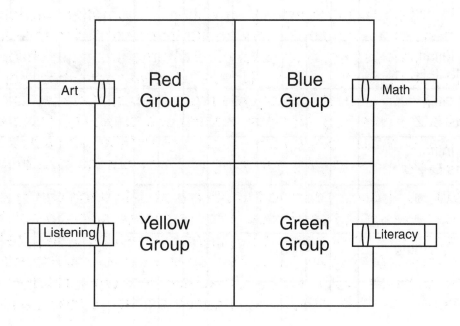

Skills Reference Chart

Skill / Activity	"Kite Tails"	"Hand in Hand"	"Letter Lane"	"Alphabet Train"	"Bunny Hop"	"Play Ball"	"In the Doghouse"	"Mail Call"	"Nuts About Letters"	"Milk & Cookies"	"Petal Power"	"Piggy Bank Bonanza"	"Monkey Business"	"Ladybug Letters"	"Consonant Crackers"	"Word Family Planets"	"Mitten Match Up"	"Word Family Wheels"	"Rhyming Concentration"
Sequencing Letters A–I	✔																		
Sequencing Letters J–Q		✔																	
Sequencing Letters R–Z			✔																
Sequencing Letters A–Z				✔	✔														
Matching Uppercase Lowercase A–I						✔													
Matching Uppercase Lowercase J–Q							✔												
Matching Uppercase Lowercase R–Z								✔											
Matching Uppercase Lowercase A–Z									✔	✔									
Identifying Initial Consonants B–H											✔								
Identifying Initial Consonants J–R												✔							
Identifying Initial Consonants S–Z													✔						
Identifying Initial Consonants B–Z														✔	✔				
Classifying Word Families																✔			
Identifying Rhyming Words																	✔		✔
Reading Word Families																		✔	

Skills Reference Chart (cont.)

Skill \\ Activity	"Letter Lace-Ups"	"Cut it Out!"	"Good Egg"	"The Name Game"	"Matching Windows"	"Lock and Key"	"Pig Poses"	"Egg-cellent Vowels"	"Pizza Party"	"By the Book"	"Lunch Break"	"Number Blocks"	"Color Sort"	"Shape Up!"	"Sight Word Snowmen"	"ABC"	"Long and Short Vowels"	"Rhyme Time"	"Colors and Numbers"
Fine Motor Development: Lacing	✔																		
Fine Motor Development: Writing			✔	✔															
Fine Motor Development: Cutting		✔																	
Visual Discrimination					✔	✔	✔												
Identify Long Vowels								✔											
Identify Short Vowels									✔										
Distinguishing Long & Short Vowels										✔	✔								
Identify Number Words												✔							
Identify Color Words													✔						
Identify Shape Words														✔					
Identify Basic Sight Words															✔				
Identify Parts of a Book: Page Numbers																✔			
Identify Parts of a Book: Author/Illustrator																	✔		
Identify Parts of a Book: Text																		✔	✔

Kite Tails

Skill: Sequencing Letters A–I

Materials: scissors; kite (page 11); kite tails (page 12); string or yarn; stapler or glue

Teacher Preparation: Cut out the kite and tails. Staple or glue a length of string or yarn to the bottom of the kite. Color and laminate the kite and tails, if desired.

(For additional practice with sequencing letters, reproduce and cut apart the letter cards in Appendix A on pages 237–239. Have the students sequence the cards or use them in games that you create.)

Kite Tails

Student Directions

1. Place the kite in front of you. Straighten the string.
2. Look at all the letters on the tails.
3. Starting with the letter A, place the tails in alphabetical order on the kite string.
4. Continue to add the tails in alphabetical order until they are all on the string.
5. Read the letters to check your work.

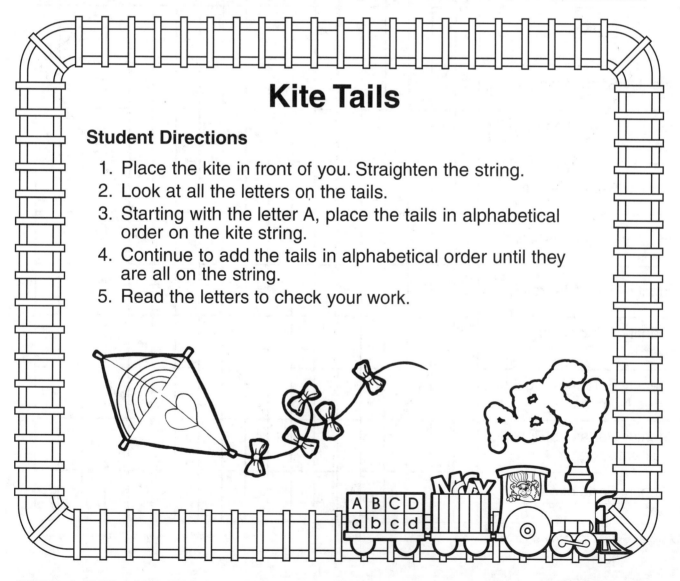

10

Kite Tails *(cont.)*

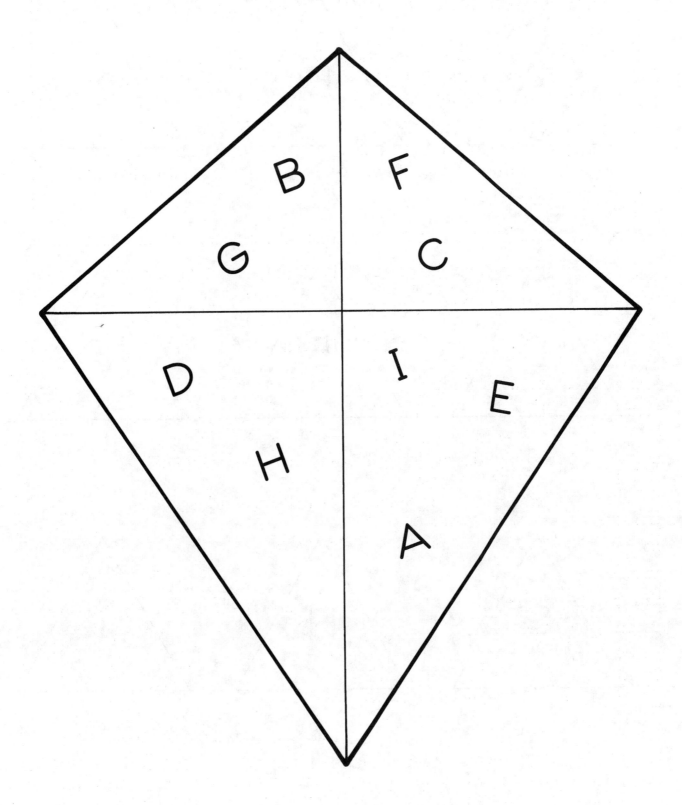

Kite Tails *(cont.)*

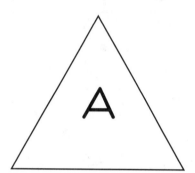 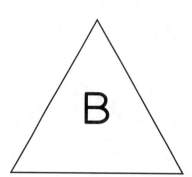 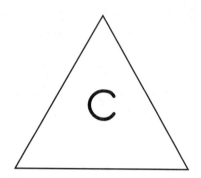

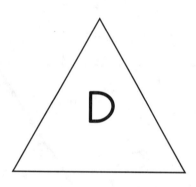 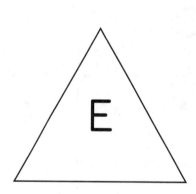 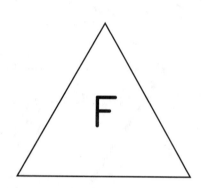

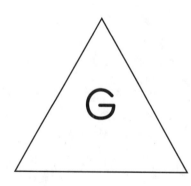 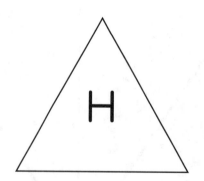 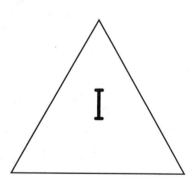

Hand in Hand

Skill: Sequencing, Letters J–Q

Materials: scissors; puzzle-pieces (pages 14 and 15)

Teacher Preparation: Cut out puzzle pieces on the dotted lines. Color and laminate pieces, if desired.

(For additional practice with sequencing letters, reproduce and cut apart the letter cards in Appendix A on pages 237–239. Have the students sequence the cards or use them in games that you create.)

Hand in Hand

Student Directions

1. Place the puzzle pieces in front of you.

2. Look at the letters. Decide which letter comes first.

3. Find the second letter and attach it to the first piece with the puzzle connection. If the piece does not fit, try again.

4. Continue until the puzzle is complete.

Hand In Hand *(cont.)*

14

Hand In Hand *(cont.)*

Letter Lane

Skill: Sequencing, Letters R–Z

Materials: scissors; houses (pages 17–18); yards (pages 19–21); transparent tape

Teacher Preparation: Cut out houses, yards and Letter Lane sign. Color and laminate houses and yards, if desired. Arrange the yards in alphabetical order according to the first letter of the picture in each yard. Attach the yards with tape to make one long street.

(For additional practice with sequencing letters, reproduce and cut apart the letter cards in Appendix A on pages 237–239. Have the students sequence the cards or use them in games that you create.)

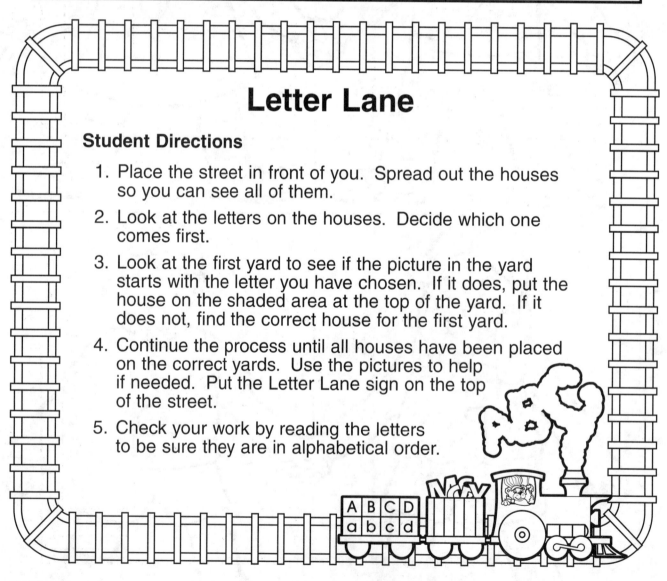

Letter Lane

Student Directions

1. Place the street in front of you. Spread out the houses so you can see all of them.

2. Look at the letters on the houses. Decide which one comes first.

3. Look at the first yard to see if the picture in the yard starts with the letter you have chosen. If it does, put the house on the shaded area at the top of the yard. If it does not, find the correct house for the first yard.

4. Continue the process until all houses have been placed on the correct yards. Use the pictures to help if needed. Put the Letter Lane sign on the top of the street.

5. Check your work by reading the letters to be sure they are in alphabetical order.

Letter Lane *(cont.)*

Letter Lane *(cont.)*

Letter Lane *(cont.)*

Letter Lane

Letter Lane *(cont.)*

20

Letter Lane *(cont.)*

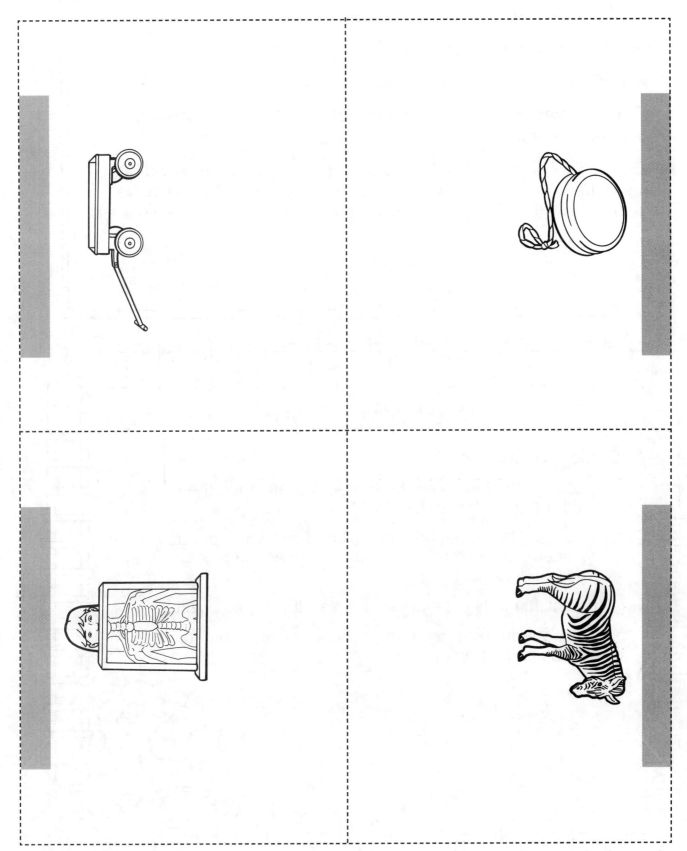

Alphabet Train

Skill: Sequencing, Letters A–Z

Materials: scissors; train puzzles (pages 23–35)

Teacher Preparation: Cut out train puzzle. Color and laminate puzzle, if desired.

(For additional practice with sequencing letters, reproduce and cut apart the letter cards in Appendix A on pages 237–239. Have the students sequence the cards or use them in games that you create.)

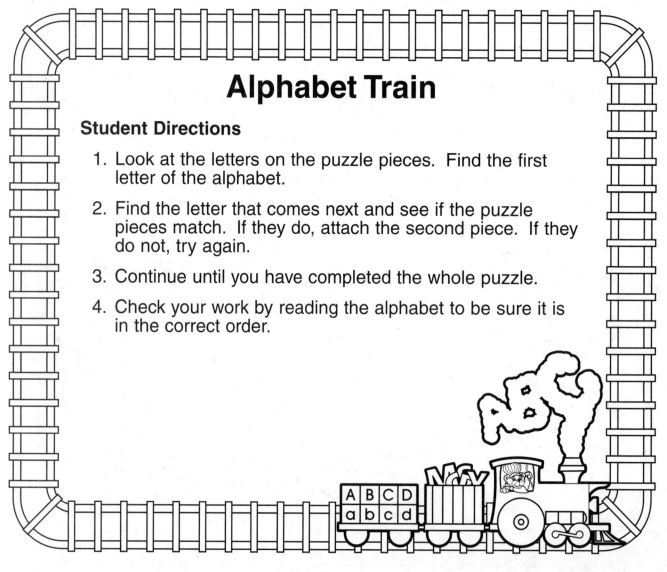

Alphabet Train

Student Directions

1. Look at the letters on the puzzle pieces. Find the first letter of the alphabet.

2. Find the letter that comes next and see if the puzzle pieces match. If they do, attach the second piece. If they do not, try again.

3. Continue until you have completed the whole puzzle.

4. Check your work by reading the alphabet to be sure it is in the correct order.

Alphabet Train *(cont.)*

Alphabet Train *(cont.)*

Alphabet Train *(cont.)*

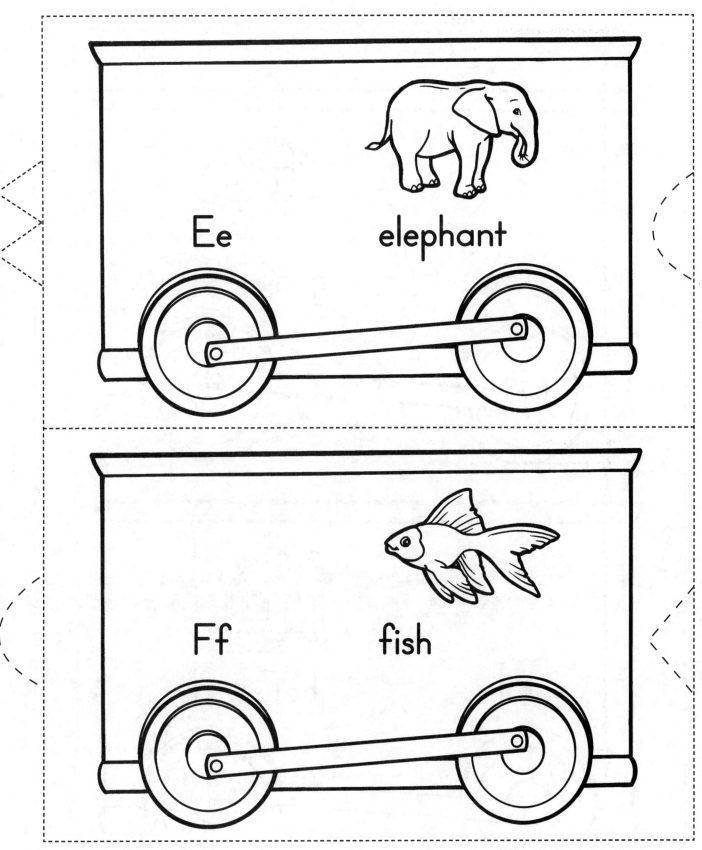

Alphabet Train (cont.)

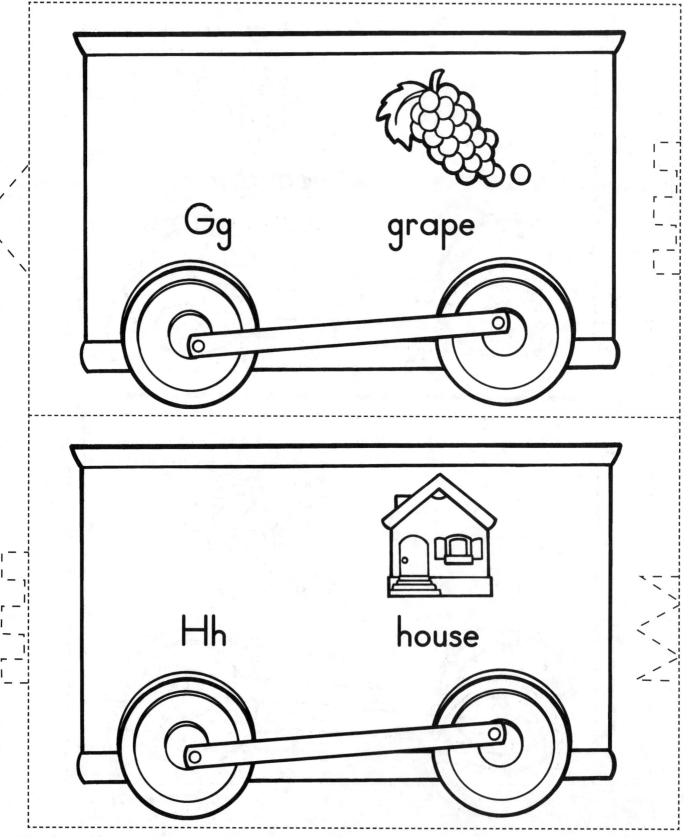

26

Alphabet Train *(cont.)*

Ii   ice cream

Jj   jar

Alphabet Train *(cont.)*

Kk   key

Ll   lion

Alphabet Train *(cont.)*

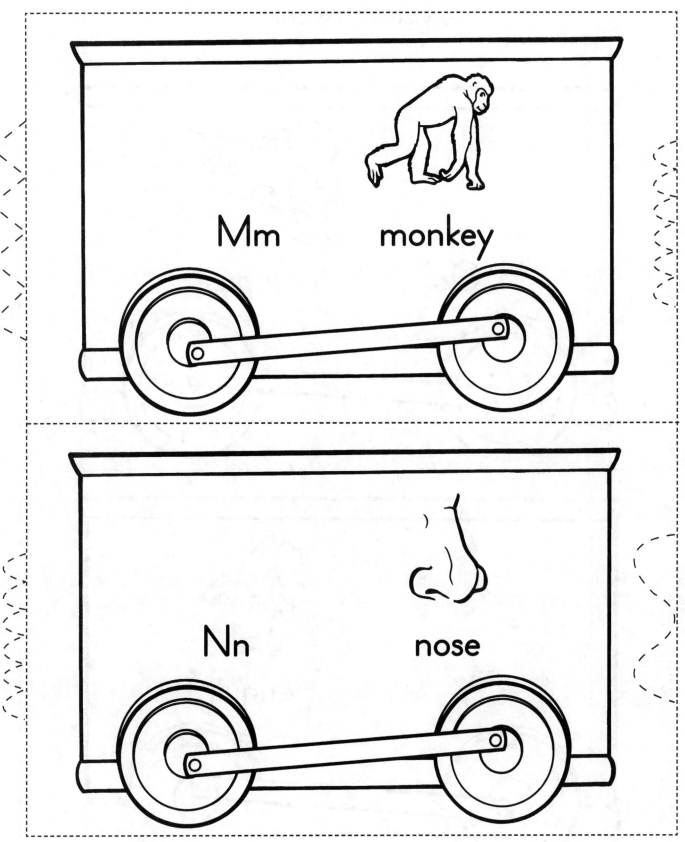

Mm   monkey

Nn   nose

Alphabet Train *(cont.)*

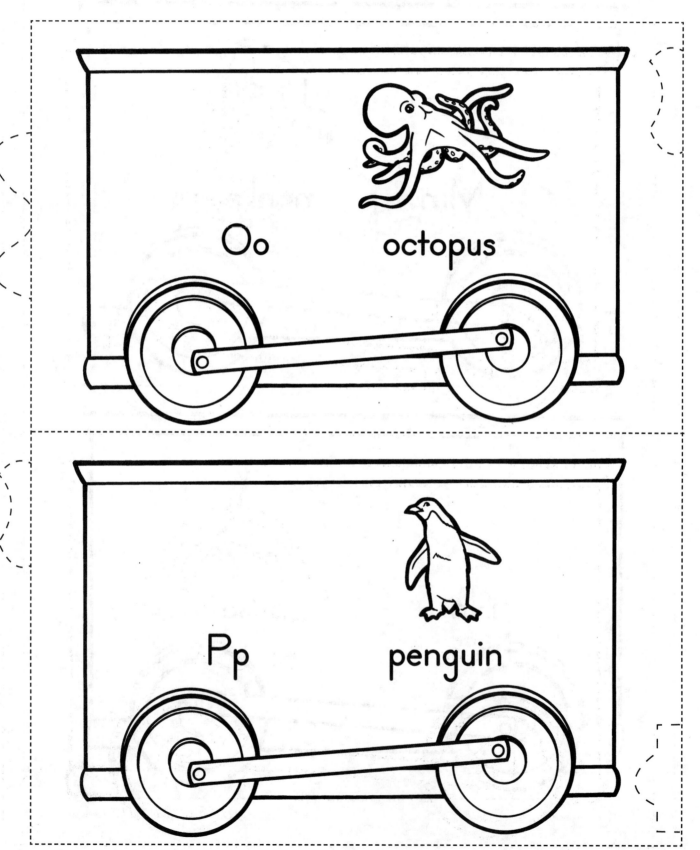

30

Alphabet Train *(cont.)*

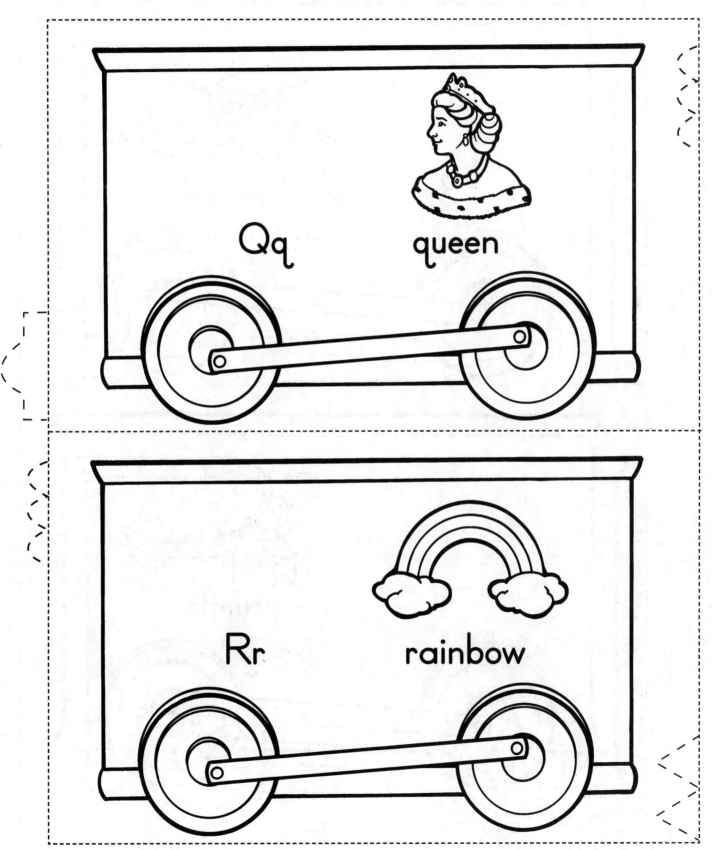

Alphabet Train *(cont.)*

Ss   snake

Tt   turtle

Alphabet Train *(cont.)*

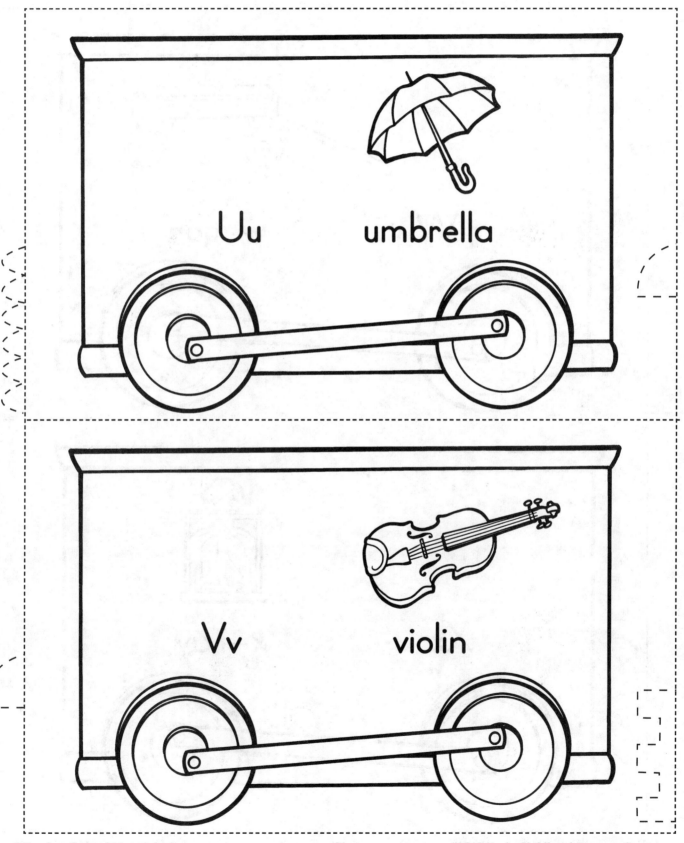

Alphabet Train *(cont.)*

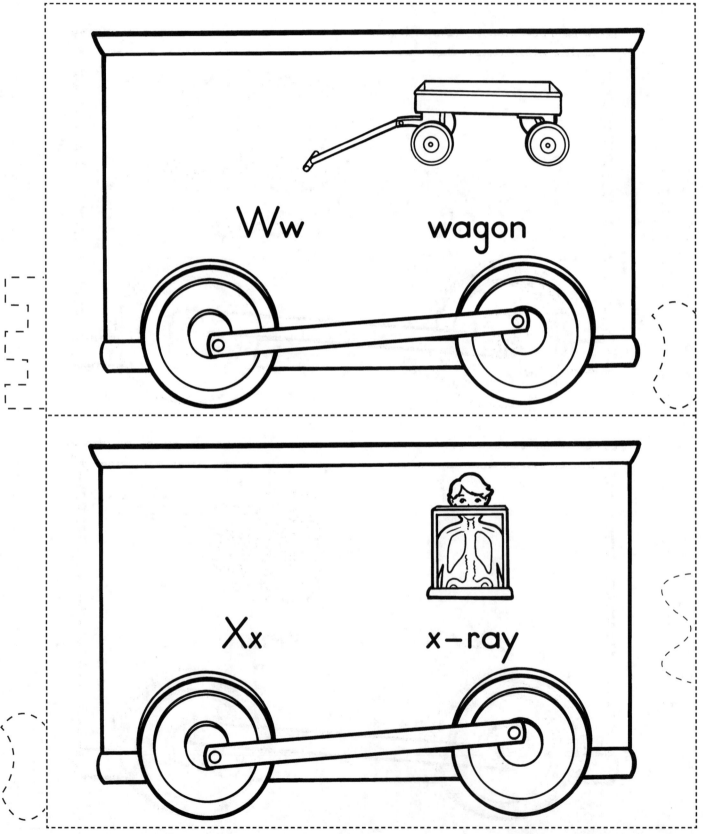

Ww   wagon

Xx   x-ray

Alphabet Train *(cont.)*

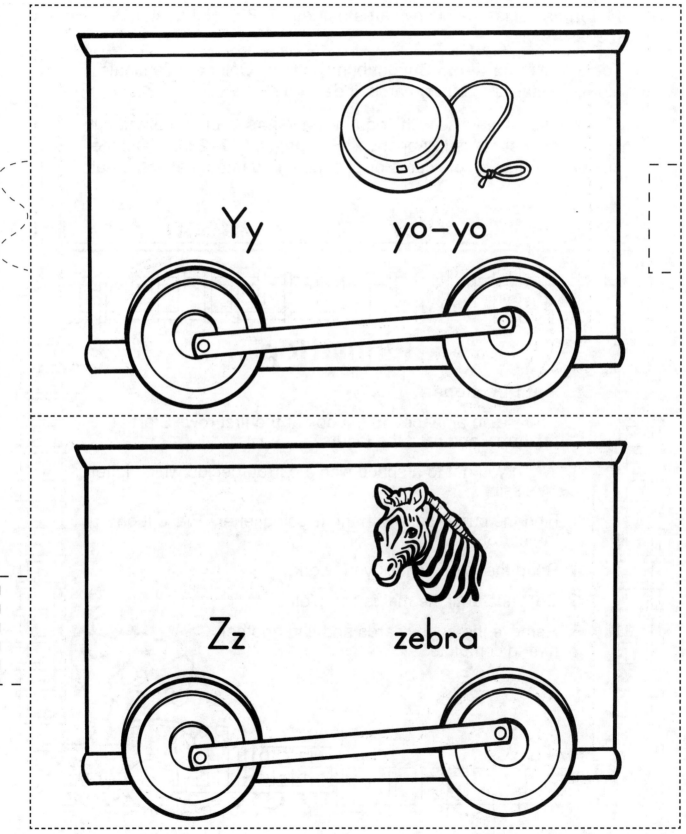

Bunny Hop

Skill: Sequencing, Letters A–Z

Materials: scissors; bunny cards (pages 37–39); alphabet mats (pages 40–42)

Teacher Preparation: Cut out bunny cards. Color and laminate alphabet mats and bunny cards, if desired.

(For additional practice with sequencing letters, reproduce and cut apart the letter cards in Appendix A on pages 237–239. Have the students sequence the cards or use them in games that you create.)

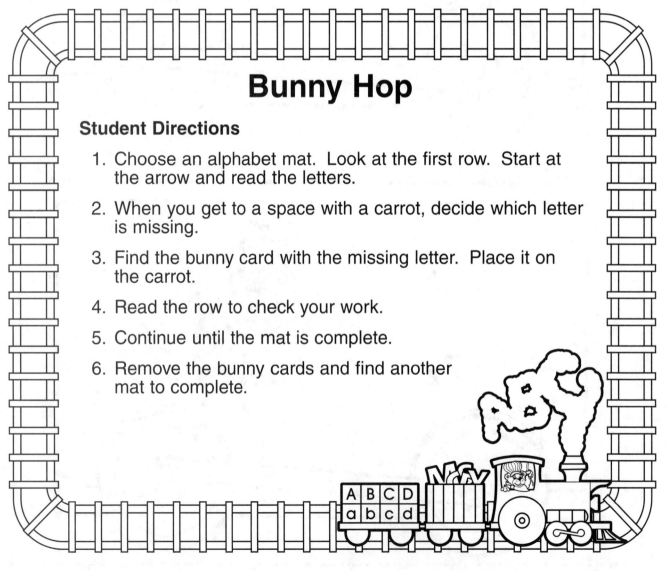

Bunny Hop

Student Directions

1. Choose an alphabet mat. Look at the first row. Start at the arrow and read the letters.

2. When you get to a space with a carrot, decide which letter is missing.

3. Find the bunny card with the missing letter. Place it on the carrot.

4. Read the row to check your work.

5. Continue until the mat is complete.

6. Remove the bunny cards and find another mat to complete.

Bunny Hop *(cont.)*

Bunny Hop *(cont.)*

Bunny Hop *(cont.)*

Bunny Hop *(cont.)*

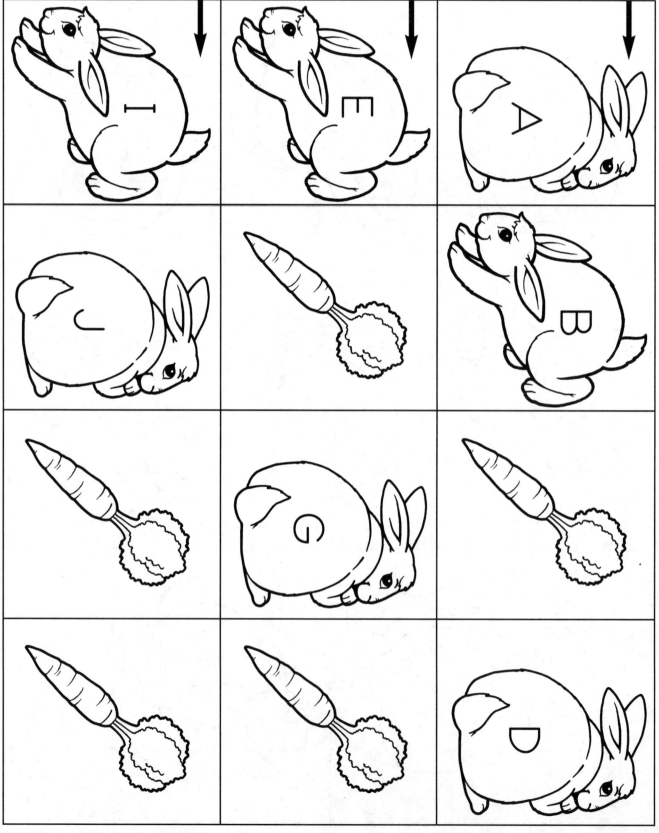

Bunny Hop *(cont.)*

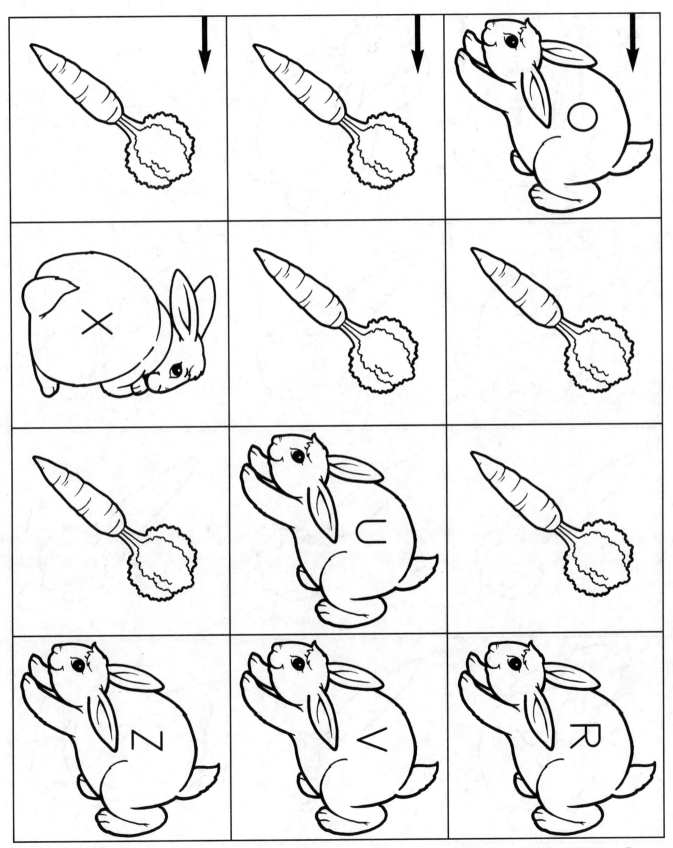

Bunny Hop *(cont.)*

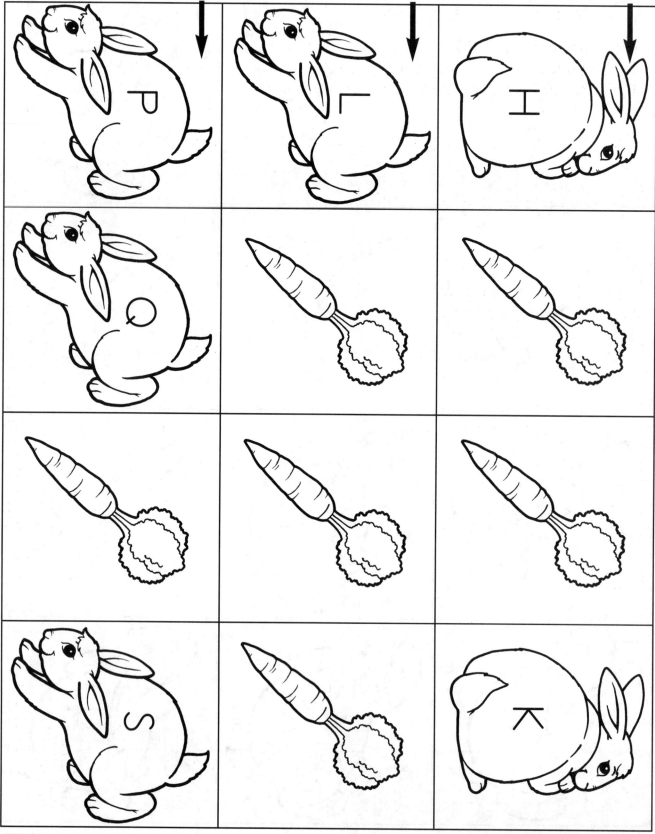

Play Ball

Skill: Matching Upper and Lowercase Letters, A–I

Materials: scissors; bats (pages 44–46); balls (page 47); pencil

Teacher Preparation: Cut out bats and balls. Write the correct lowercase letter on the back of each bat for student self-checking. Color and laminate bats and balls, if desired.

Play Ball

Student Directions

1. Choose a bat and look at the letter on it.

2. Look at the balls. Find the lowercase letter that matches the letter on the bat. Place the ball and bat together.

3. Choose another bat and repeat the process until all the bats and balls are matched.

4. To check your work, look at the lowercase letters written on the back of the bats to see if they match the balls.

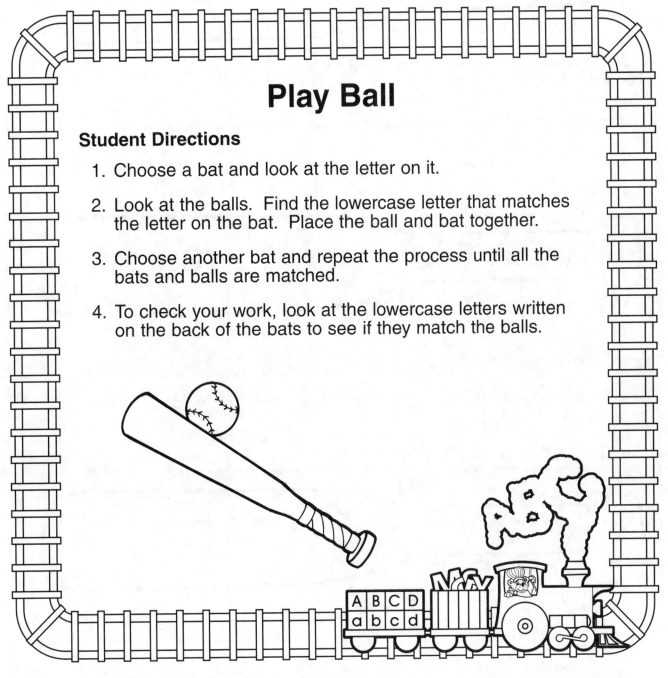

Play Ball *(cont.)*

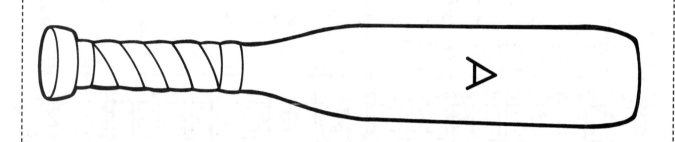

44

Play Ball *(cont.)*

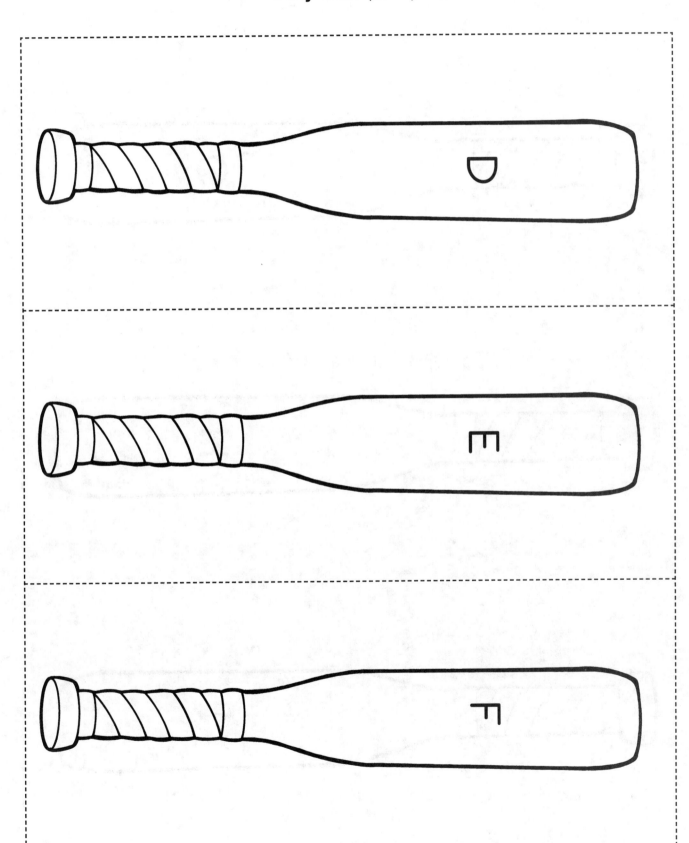

Play Ball *(cont.)*

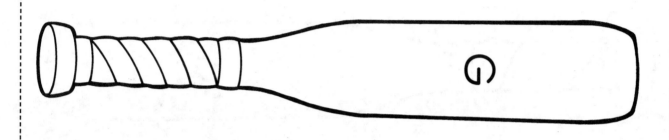

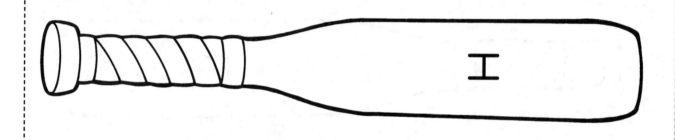

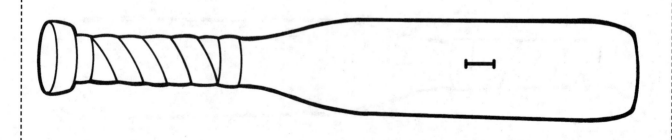

Play Ball *(cont.)*

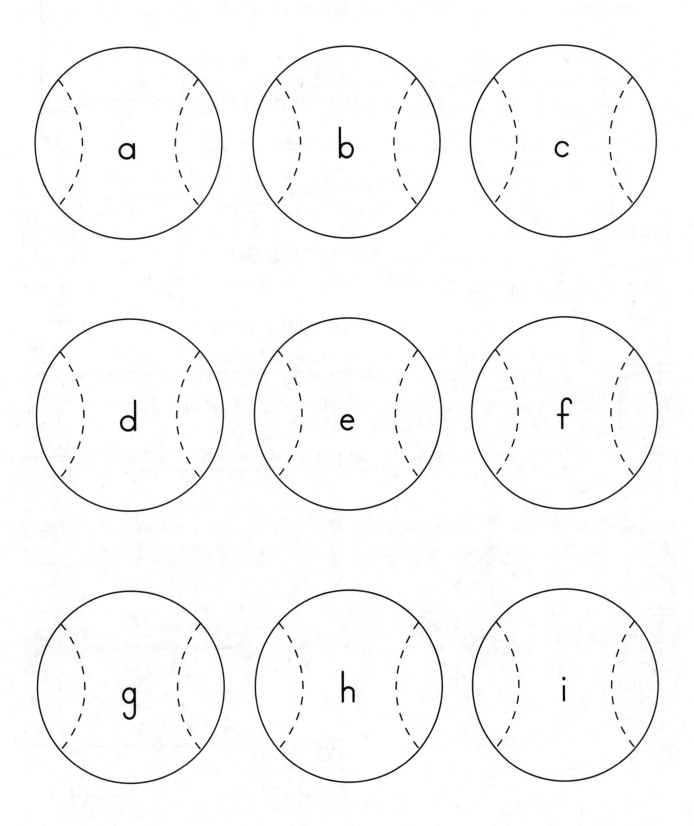

In the Doghouse

Skill: Matching Upper and Lowercase Letters, J–Q

Materials: scissors; doghouses (pages 49 and 50); dogs (page 51); pencil

Teacher Preparation: Cut out the doghouses and dogs. Write the corresponding lowercase letter on the back of each doghouse for student self-checking. Color and laminate doghouses and dogs, if desired.

In the Doghouse

Student Directions

1. Choose a doghouse and look at the letter on it.

2. Find a dog with a lowercase letter that matches the letter on the doghouse. Put the dog in the doghouse.

3. Choose another doghouse and continue until all doghouses and dogs are matched.

4. To check your work, look at the lowercase letters written on the backs of the doghouses to see if they match the dogs.

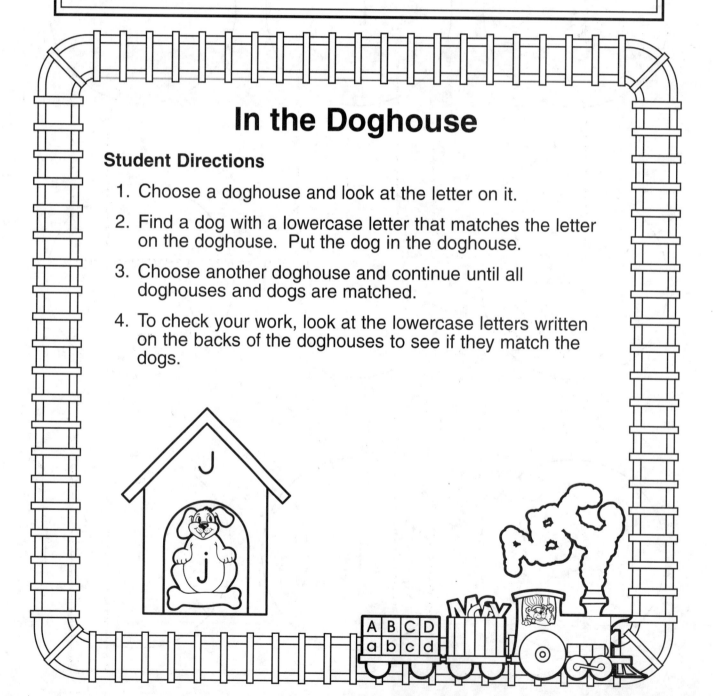

In the Doghouse *(cont.)*

In the Doghouse *(cont.)*

In the Doghouse *(cont.)*

Mail Call

Skill: Matching Upper and Lowercase Letters, R–Z

Materials: scissors; mailboxes (pages 53–55); envelopes (pages 56 and 57); pencil

Teacher Preparation: Cut out mailboxes and envelopes. Write the corresponding lowercase letter on the back of each mailbox for student self-checking. Color and laminate the mailboxes and envelopes, if desired.

Mail Call

Student Directions

1. Spread out the mailboxes and envelopes in front of you.

2. Choose an envelope. Look at the lowercase letter on it. Find the mailbox with the matching uppercase letter. Put the envelope on the mailbox.

3. Continue until all envelopes have been matched with the correct mailboxes.

4. To check your work, look at the lowercase letter written on the backs of the mailboxes to see if they match the envelopes.

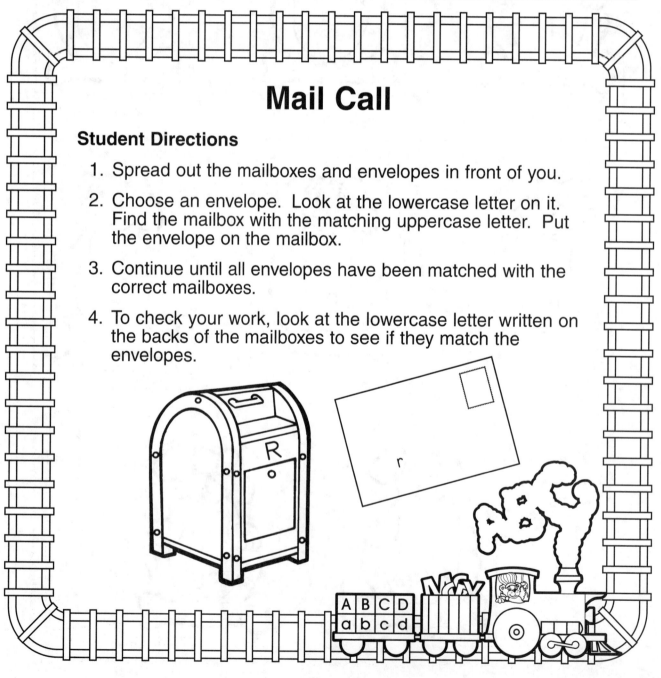

52

Mail Call *(cont.)*

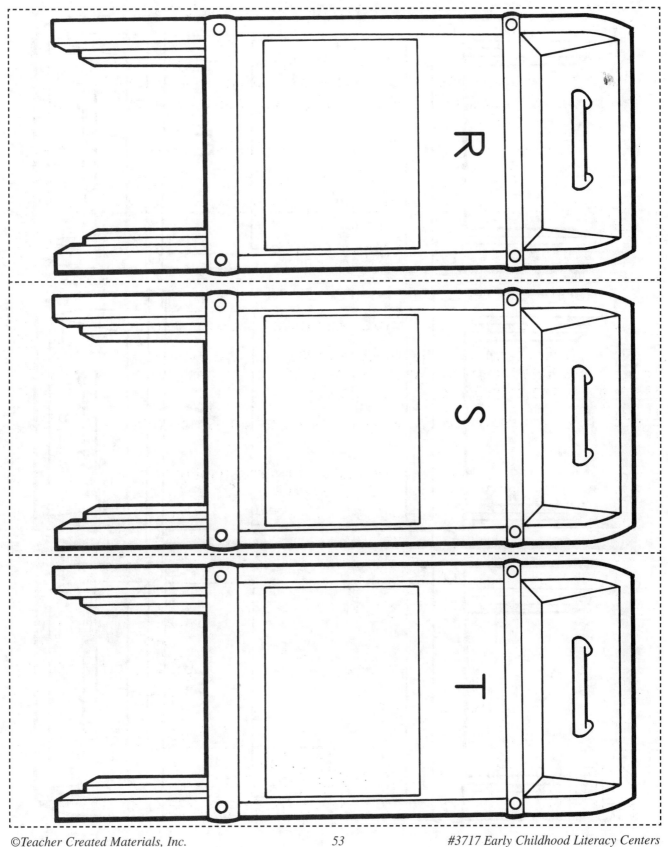

Mail Call *(cont.)*

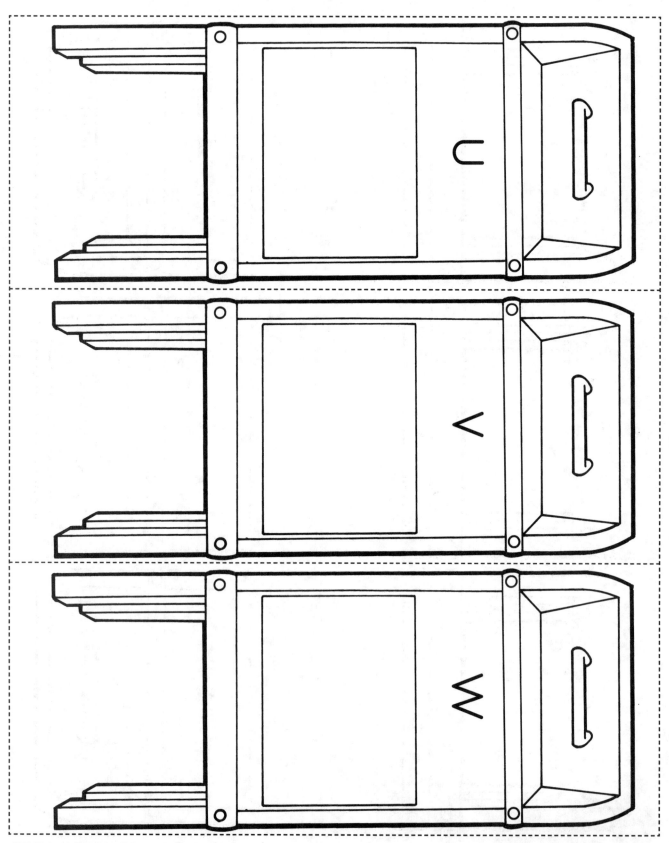

54

Mail Call *(cont.)*

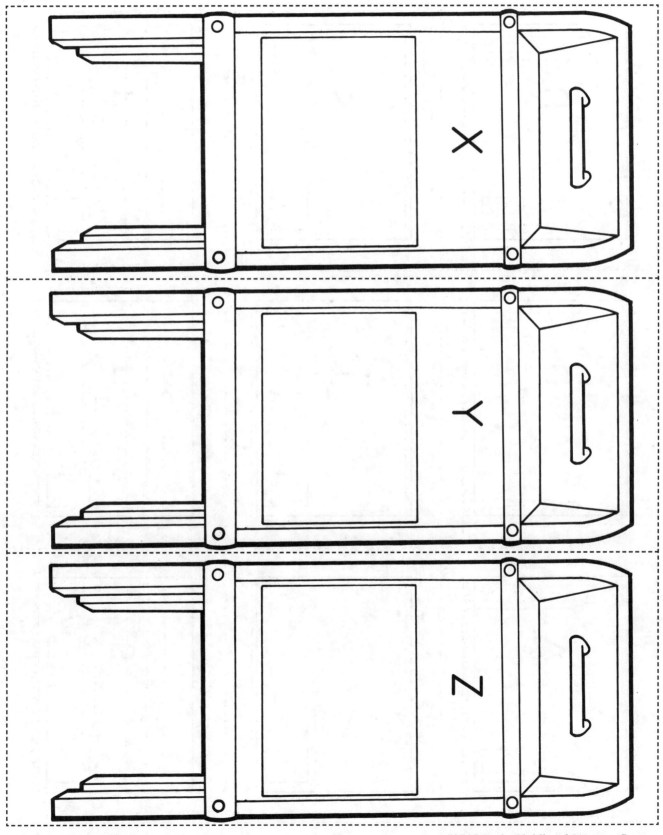

Mail Call *(cont.)*

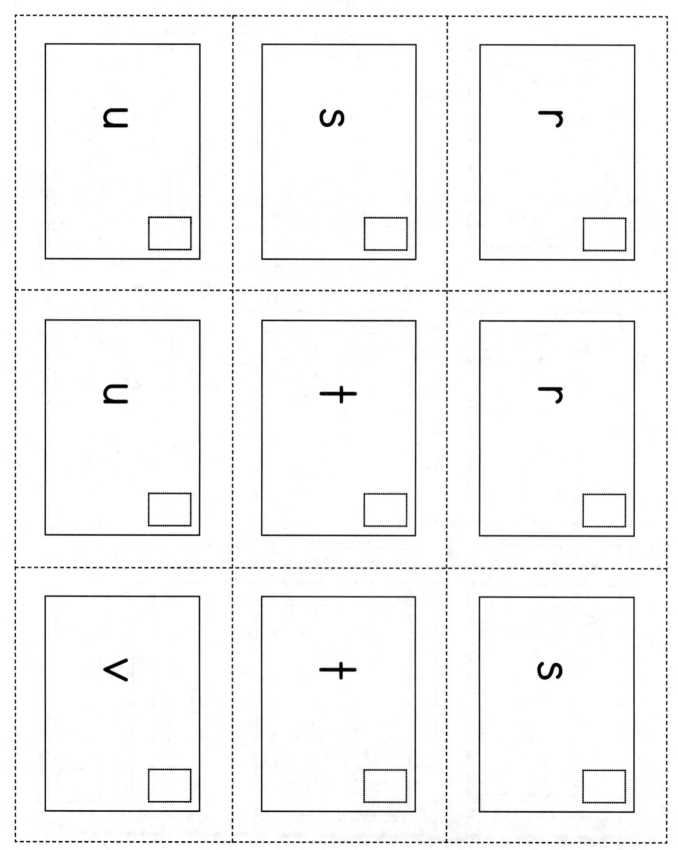

56

Mail Call *(cont.)*

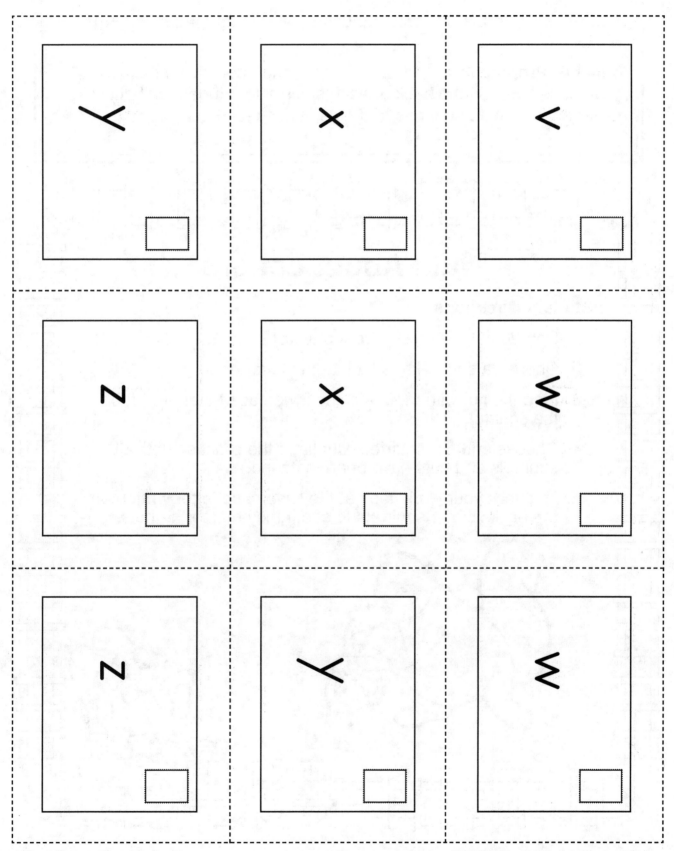

Nuts About Letters

Skill: Matching Upper and Lowercase Letters, A–Z

Materials: scissors; squirrels (pages 59–65); nuts (pages 65–66); pencil

Teacher Preparation: Cut out squirrels and nuts. Write the lowercase letter on the back of each squirrel for student self-checking. Color and laminate squirrels and nuts, if desired.

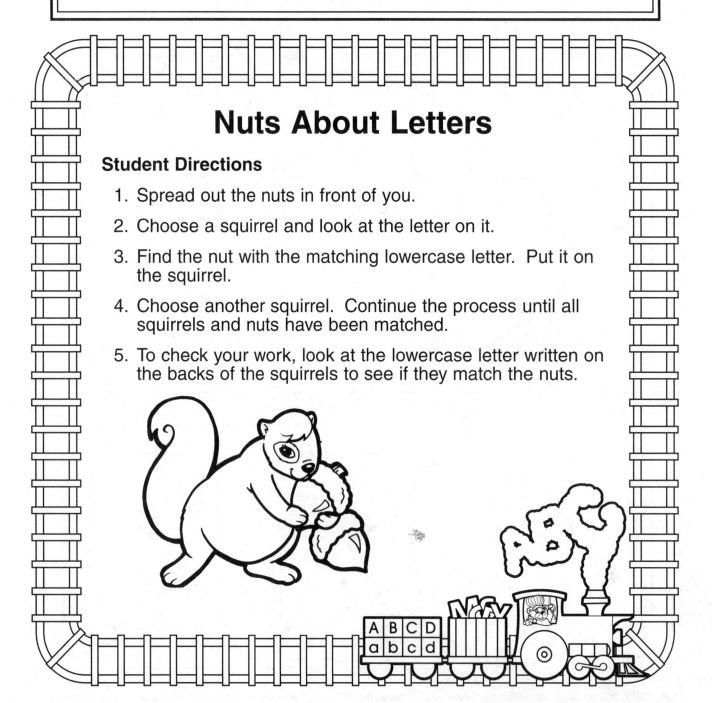

Nuts About Letters

Student Directions

1. Spread out the nuts in front of you.

2. Choose a squirrel and look at the letter on it.

3. Find the nut with the matching lowercase letter. Put it on the squirrel.

4. Choose another squirrel. Continue the process until all squirrels and nuts have been matched.

5. To check your work, look at the lowercase letter written on the backs of the squirrels to see if they match the nuts.

58

Nuts About Letters *(cont.)*

Nuts About Letters *(cont.)*

Nuts About Letters *(cont.)*

Nuts About Letters *(cont.)*

Nuts About Letters *(cont.)*

Nuts About Letters *(cont.)*

Nuts About Letters *(cont.)*

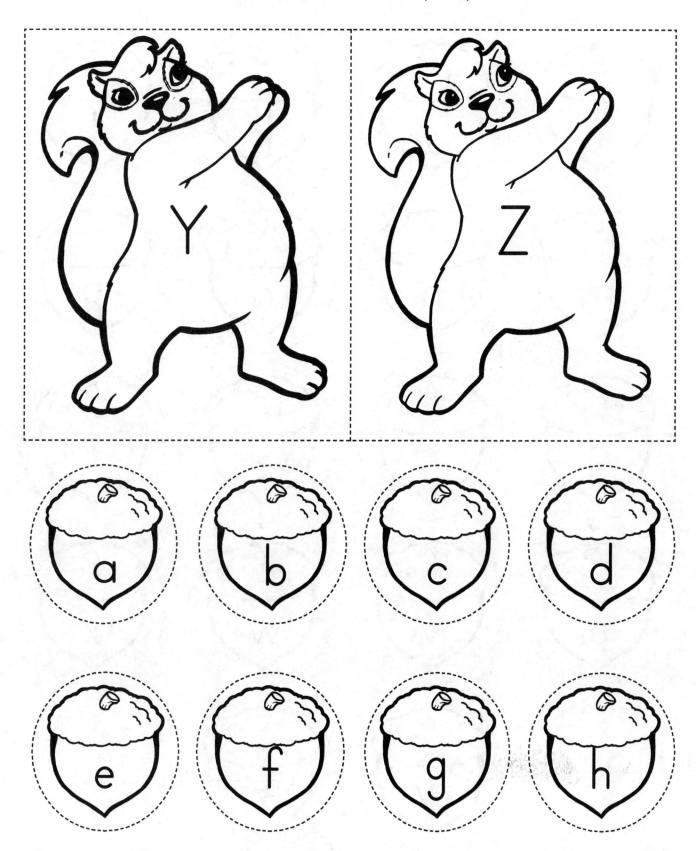

Nuts About Letters *(cont.)*

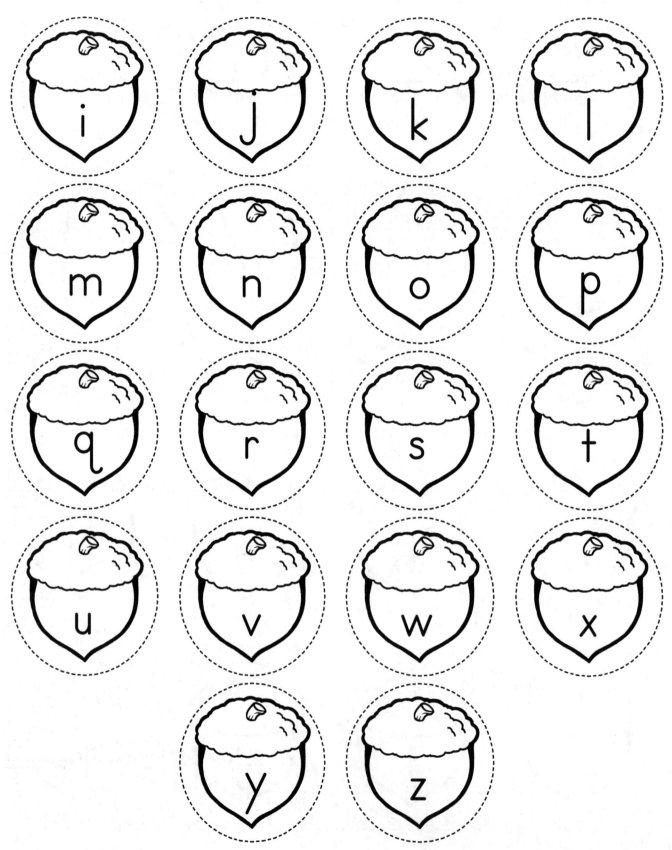

Milk and Cookies

Skill: Matching Upper and Lowercase Letters, A–Z

Materials: scissors; milk and plate cards (pages 68–74); cookies (pages 74–76); pencil

Teacher Preparation: Cut out milk card and cookies. Write the lowercase letter on the back of each glass of milk for student self-checking. Color and laminate milk and cookies, if desired.

Milk and Cookies

Student Directions

1. Spread out the cookies in front of you.

2. Choose one milk and plate card. Look at the letter on the glass.

3. Find two cookies that have a matching lowercase letter. Put them on the plate.

4. Choose another card. Continue until all glasses of milk and cookies have been matched.

5. To check your work, look at the lowercase letters written on the back of each card to see if they match the cookies.

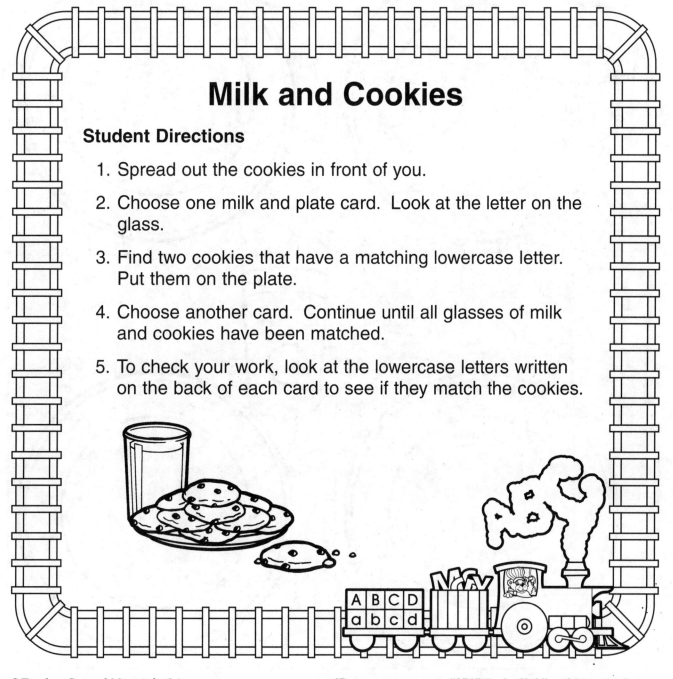

Milk and Cookies *(cont.)*

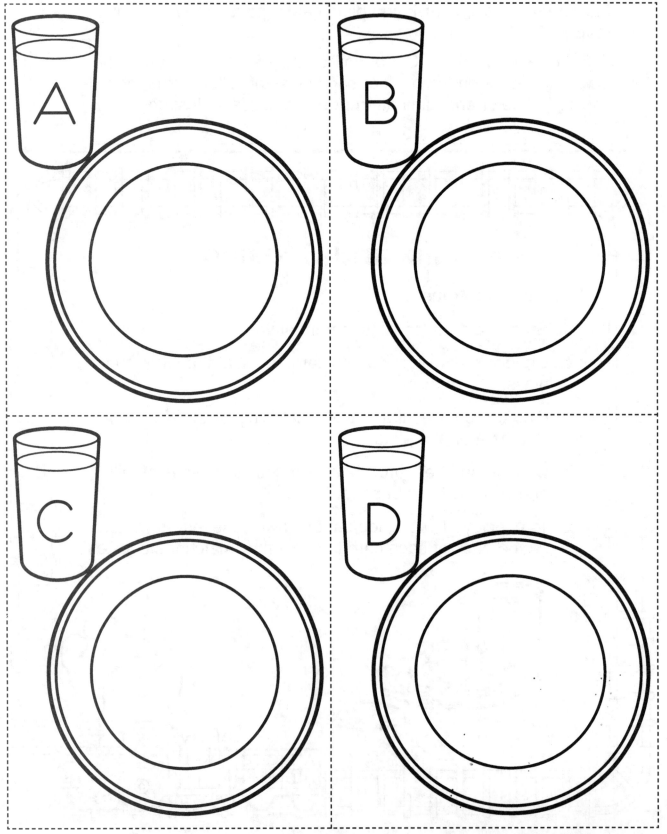

Milk and Cookies *(cont.)*

Milk and Cookies *(cont.)*

Milk and Cookies *(cont.)*

Milk and Cookies *(cont.)*

Milk and Cookies *(cont.)*

Milk and Cookies *(cont.)*

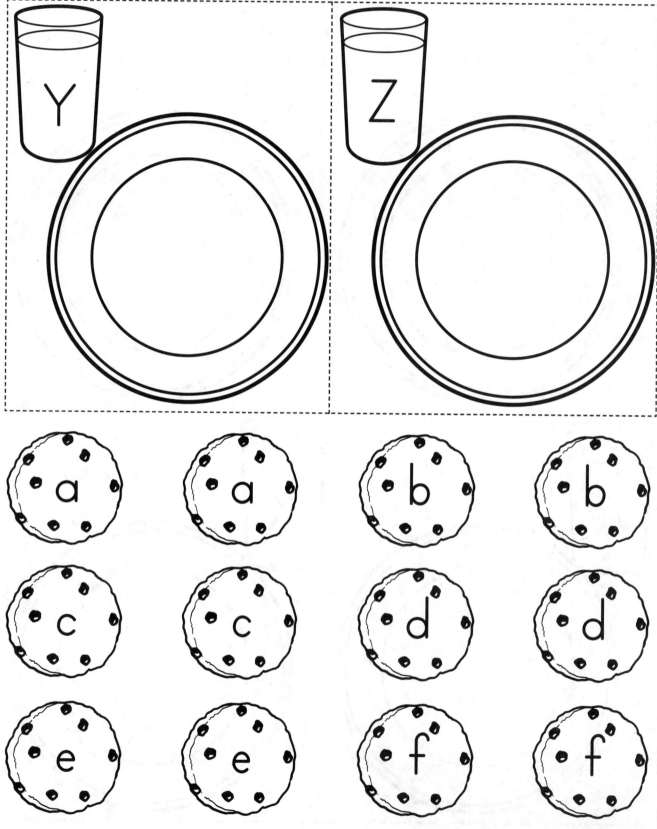

Milk and Cookies *(cont.)*

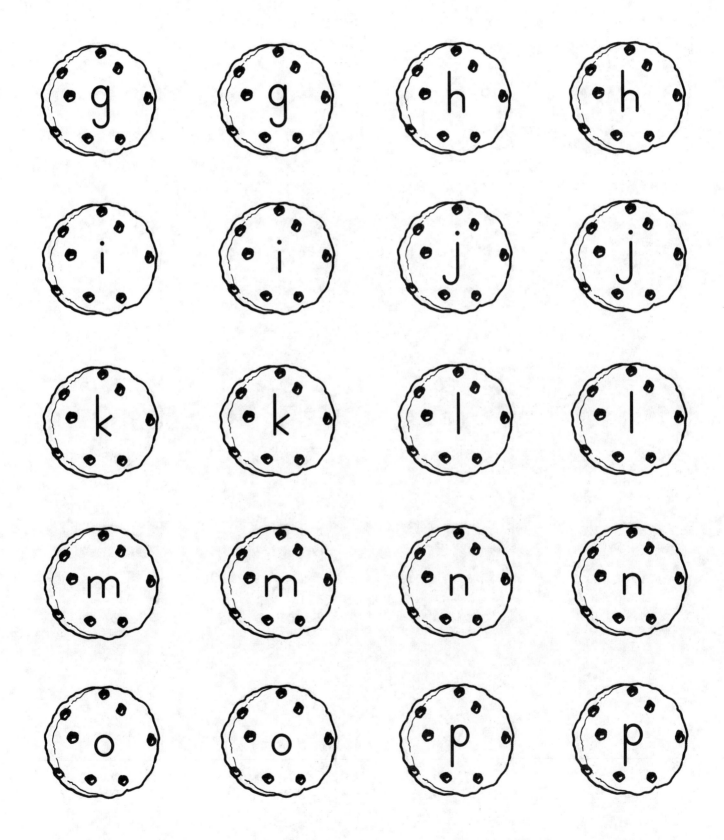

Milk and Cookies *(cont.)*

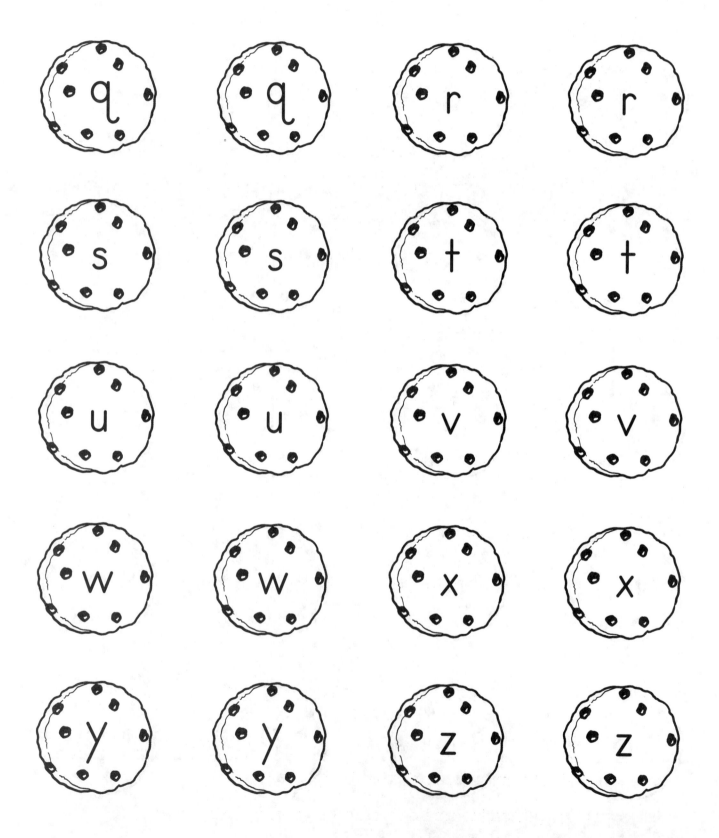

Petal Power

Skill: Identifying Initial Consonants, B–H

Materials: scissors; flowers (pages 78 and 80); petals (pages 79 and 81); pencil

Teacher Preparation: Cut out petals. Write the correct initial consonant on the back of each petal for student self-checking. Color and laminate petals and flowers, if desired.

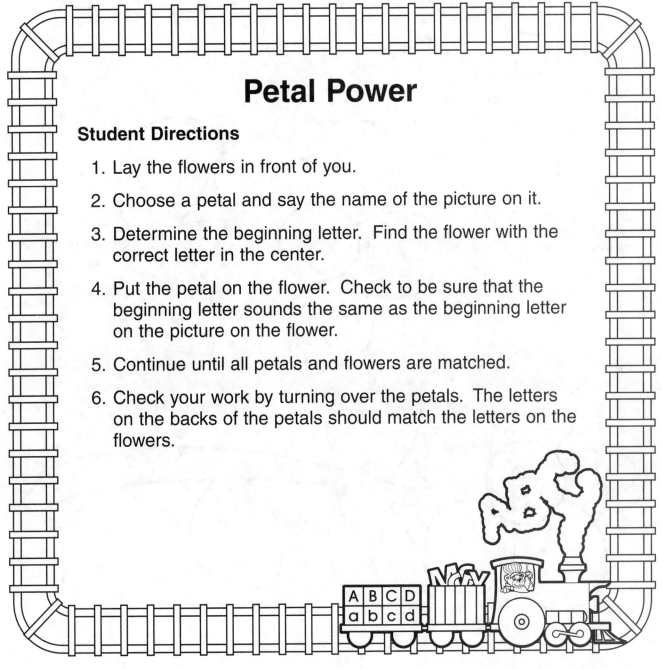

Petal Power

Student Directions

1. Lay the flowers in front of you.

2. Choose a petal and say the name of the picture on it.

3. Determine the beginning letter. Find the flower with the correct letter in the center.

4. Put the petal on the flower. Check to be sure that the beginning letter sounds the same as the beginning letter on the picture on the flower.

5. Continue until all petals and flowers are matched.

6. Check your work by turning over the petals. The letters on the backs of the petals should match the letters on the flowers.

Petal Power *(cont.)*

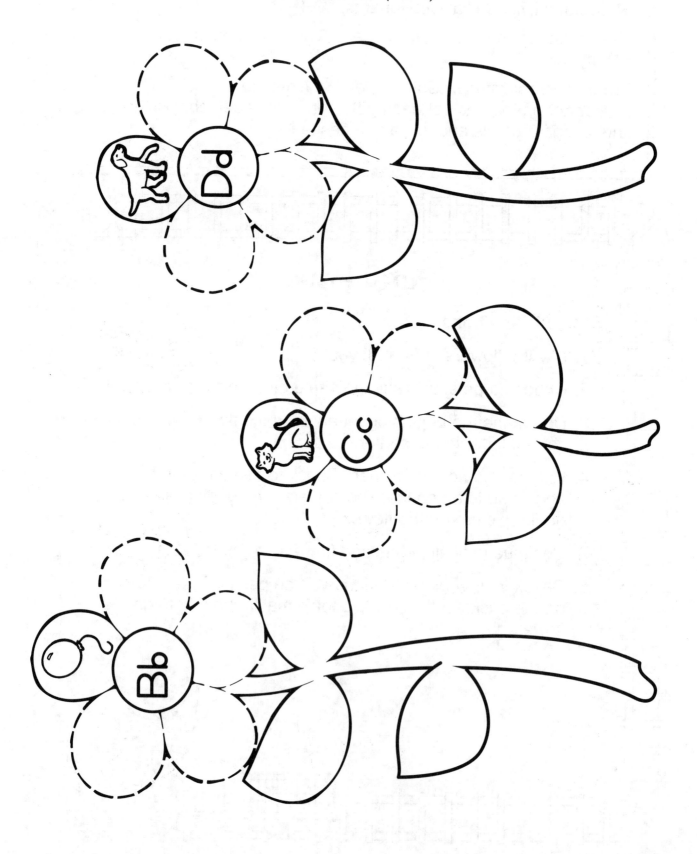

78

Petal Power *(cont.)*

Petal Power *(cont.)*

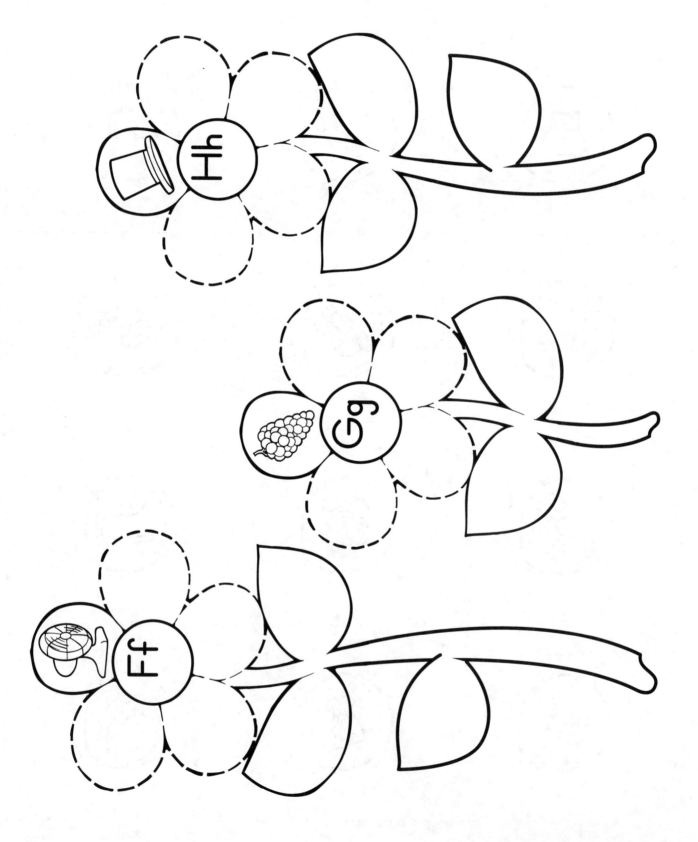

Petal Power *(cont.)*

Piggy Bank Bonanza

Skill: Identifying Initial Consonants, J–R

Materials: scissors; piggy banks (pages 83–86); coins (pages 87–88); pencil

Teacher Preparation: Cut out piggy banks and coins. Write the correct initial consonant on the back of each coin for student self-checking. Color and laminate piggy banks and coins, if desired.

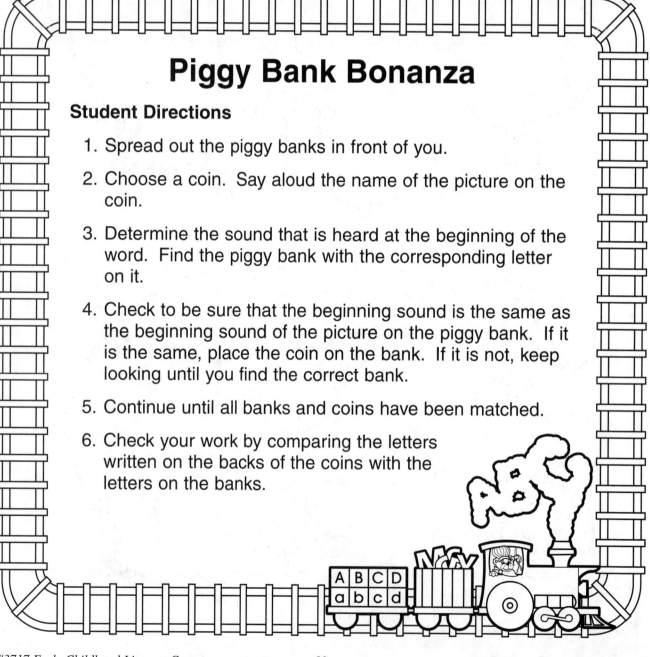

Piggy Bank Bonanza

Student Directions

1. Spread out the piggy banks in front of you.

2. Choose a coin. Say aloud the name of the picture on the coin.

3. Determine the sound that is heard at the beginning of the word. Find the piggy bank with the corresponding letter on it.

4. Check to be sure that the beginning sound is the same as the beginning sound of the picture on the piggy bank. If it is the same, place the coin on the bank. If it is not, keep looking until you find the correct bank.

5. Continue until all banks and coins have been matched.

6. Check your work by comparing the letters written on the backs of the coins with the letters on the banks.

Piggy Bank Bonanza *(cont.)*

Piggy Bank Bonanza *(cont.)*

84

Piggy Bank Bonanza *(cont.)*

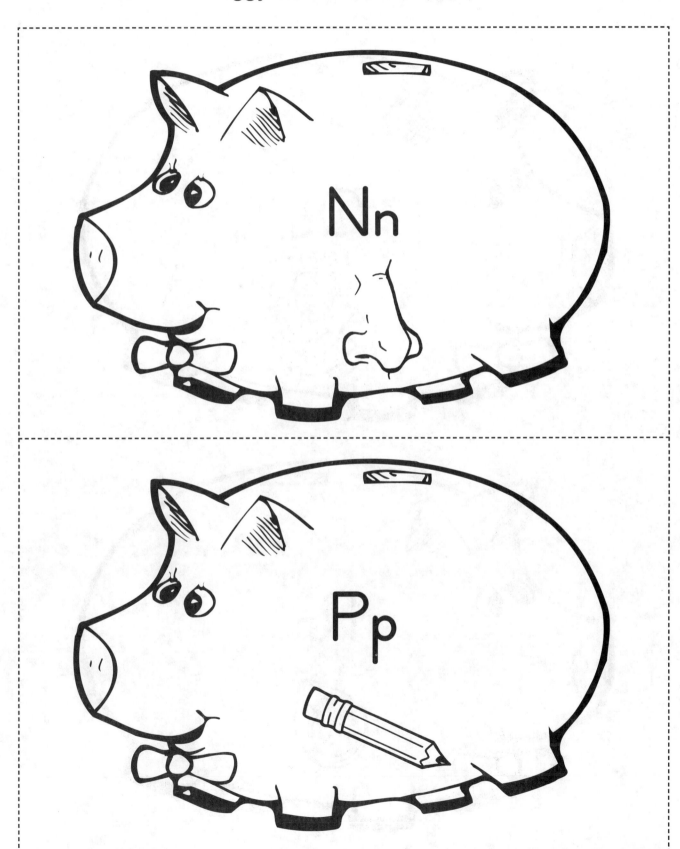

Piggy Bank Bonanza *(cont.)*

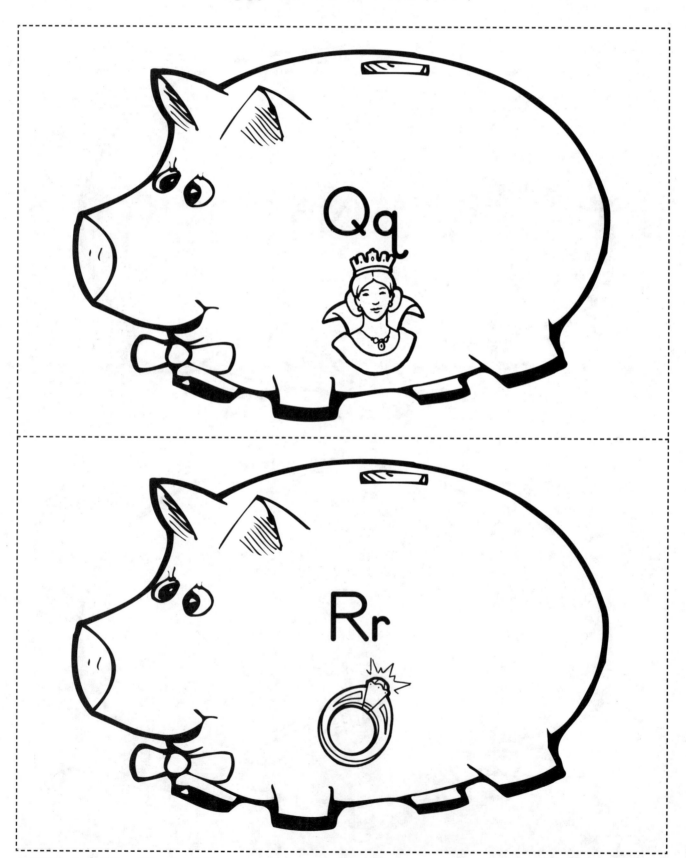

86

Piggy Bank Bonanza *(cont.)*

Piggy Bank Bonanza *(cont.)*

Monkey Business

Skill: Identifying Initial Consonants, S–Z

Materials: scissors; monkeys (pages 90–91); bananas (page 92); pencil

Teacher Preparation: Cut out monkey cards and bananas. Write the initial consonant on the back of each banana for student self-checking. Color and laminate cards and bananas, if desired.

Monkey Business

Student Directions

1. Spread out the bananas in front of you.

2. Choose a monkey card. Look at the letter on it. Determine the sound of the letter.

3. Look at the bananas. Find two bananas beginning with the same sound. Place the bananas with the corresponding monkey.

4. Choose another monkey card. Continue until all of the bananas have been matched with the correct monkey.

5. To check your work, look at the letters on the backs of the bananas to see if they match the letters on the monkeys.

Monkey Business *(cont.)*

Monkey Business *(cont.)*

Monkey Business *(cont.)*

92

Ladybug Letters

Skill: Identifying Initial Consonants, B–Z

Materials: scissors; ladybugs (pages 94–99); spots (pages 99–101); pencil

Teacher Preparation: Cut out ladybugs and spots. Write the initial consonant on the back of each spot for student self-checking. Color and laminate the ladybugs and spots, if desired.

Ladybug Letters

Student Directions

1. Spread out the ladybugs in front of you.

2. Choose a spot. Say the name of the picture aloud.

3. Determine the sound you hear at the beginning of the word. Find the ladybug that has the matching letter on it. Put the spot on the ladybug inside the oval.

4. Choose another spot and continue until all ladybugs have two spots.

5. Check your work by comparing the letters on the backs of the spots to the letters on the ladybugs.

Ladybug Letters *(cont.)*

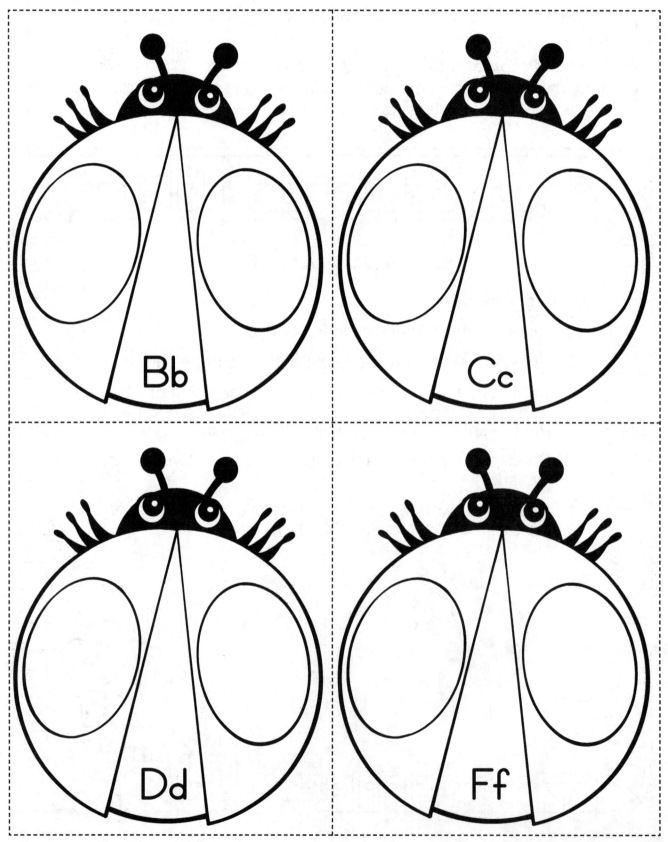

Ladybug Letters *(cont.)*

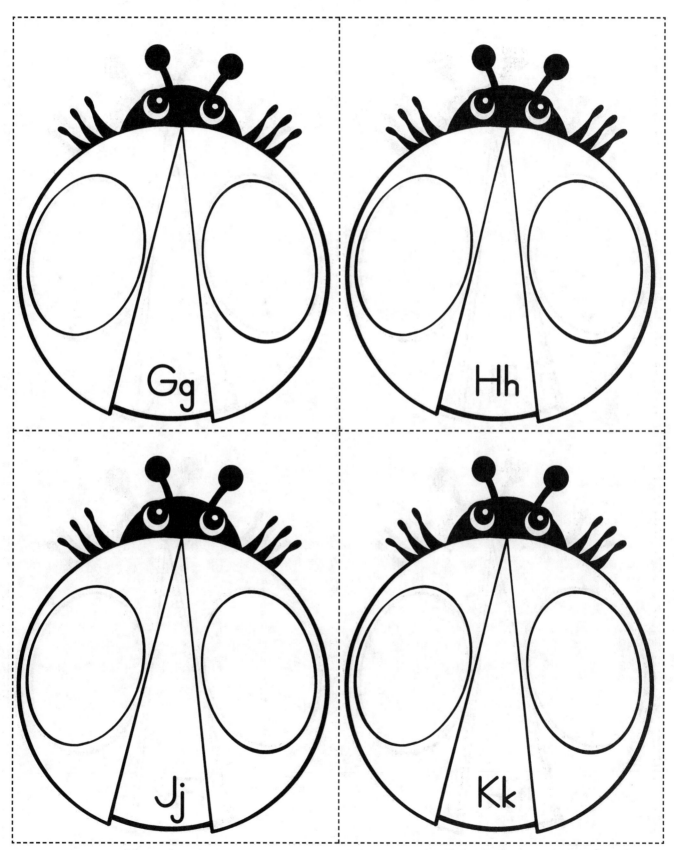

Ladybug Letters *(cont.)*

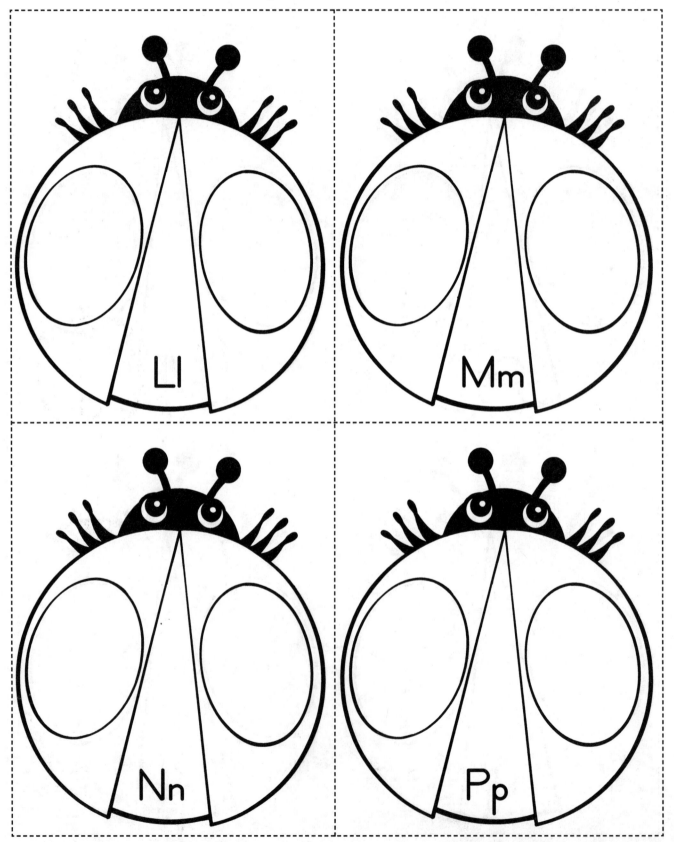

Ladybug Letters *(cont.)*

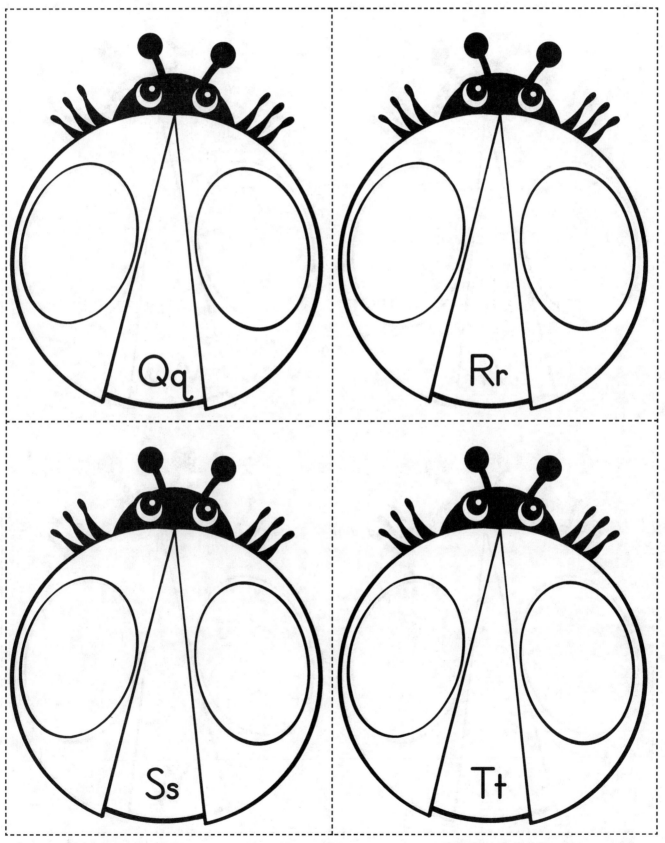

Ladybug Letters *(cont.)*

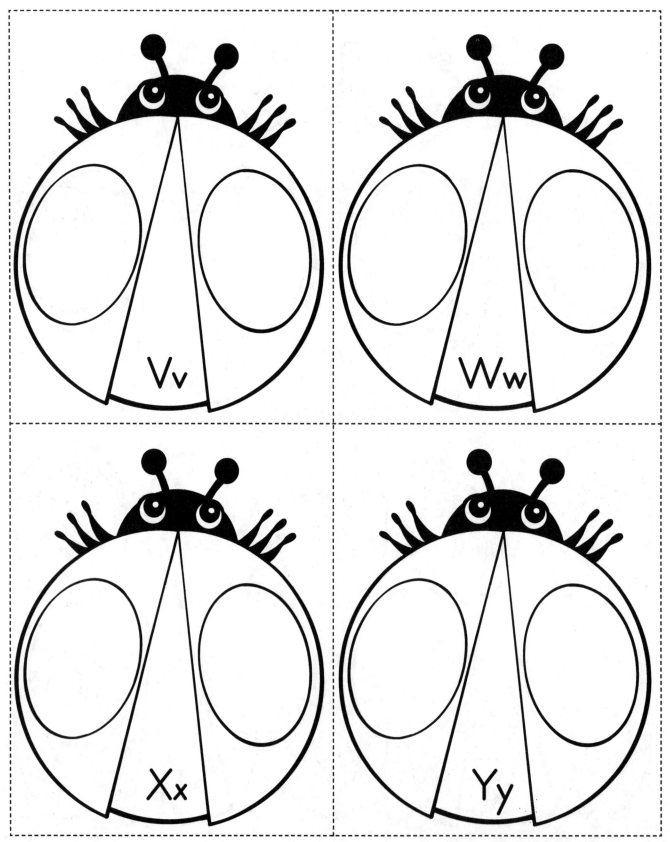

98

Ladybug Letters *(cont.)*

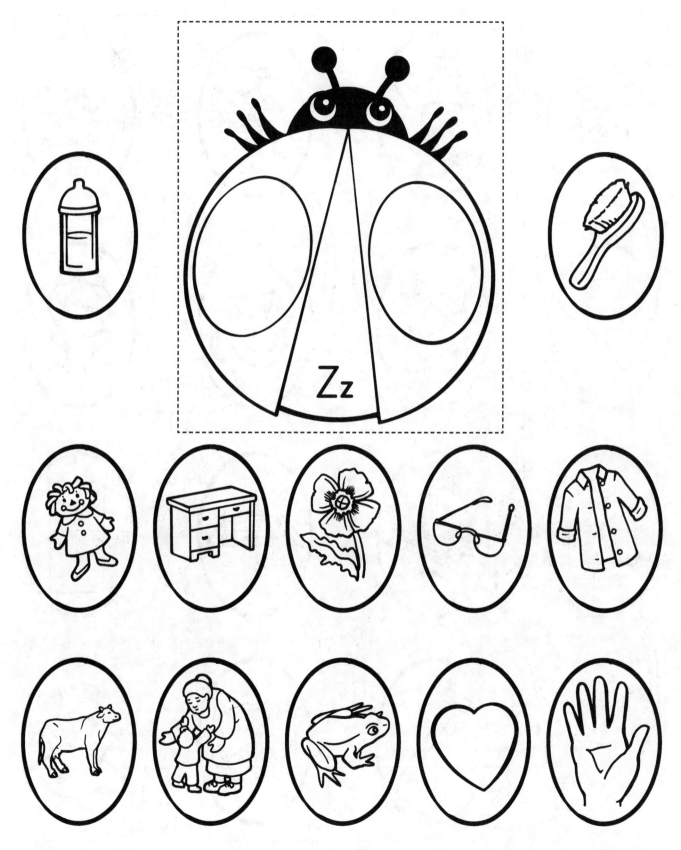

Ladybug Letters *(cont.)*

Ladybug Letters *(cont.)*

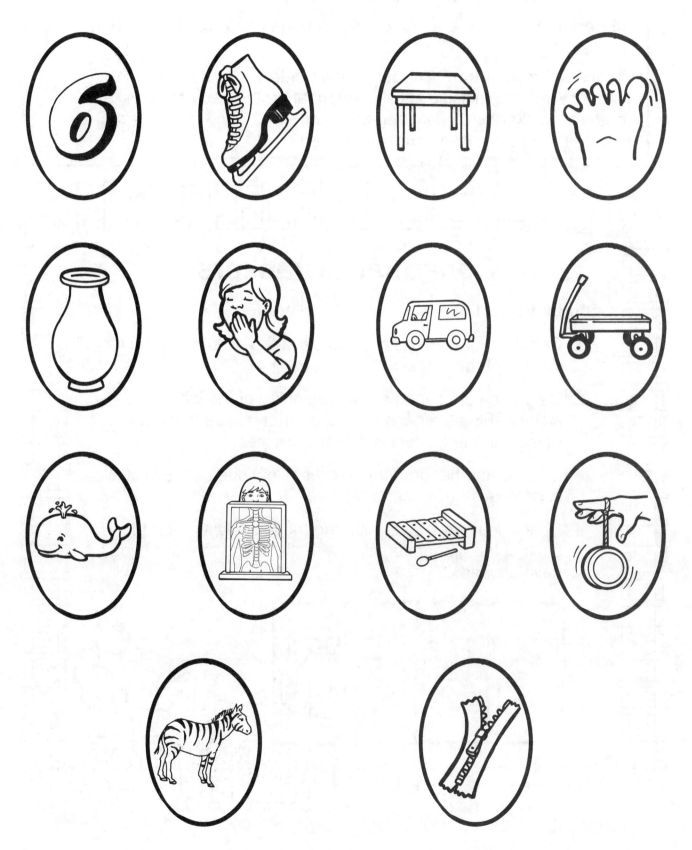

Consonant Crackers

Skill: Identifying Initial Consonants

Materials: scissors; graham crackers (pages 103–106); consonant cards (pages 106–107); pencil

Teacher Preparation: Cut out graham crackers and consonant cards. Write the missing initial consonant on the back of each graham cracker for student self-checking. Color and laminate graham crackers and consonant cards, if desired.

Consonant Crackers

Student Directions

1. Choose a graham cracker. Look at the picture in the last section of the cracker.

2. Determine the sound at the beginning of the word in the picture. Find the consonant card that makes that sound. Place it in the first section of the cracker.

3. Choose another graham cracker. Continue until all initial consonants have been matched.

4. Check your work by comparing the letter written on the back of the graham cracker with the consonant card you have chosen.

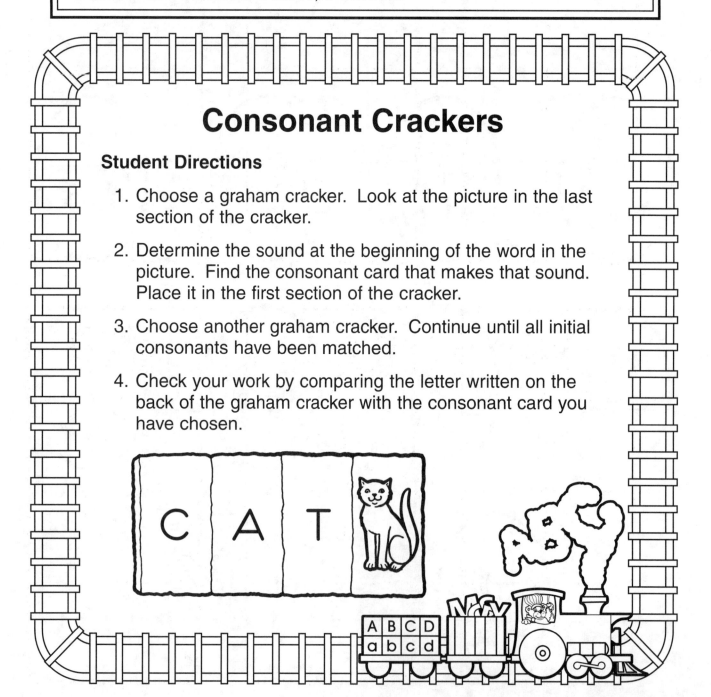

102

Consonant Crackers *(cont.)*

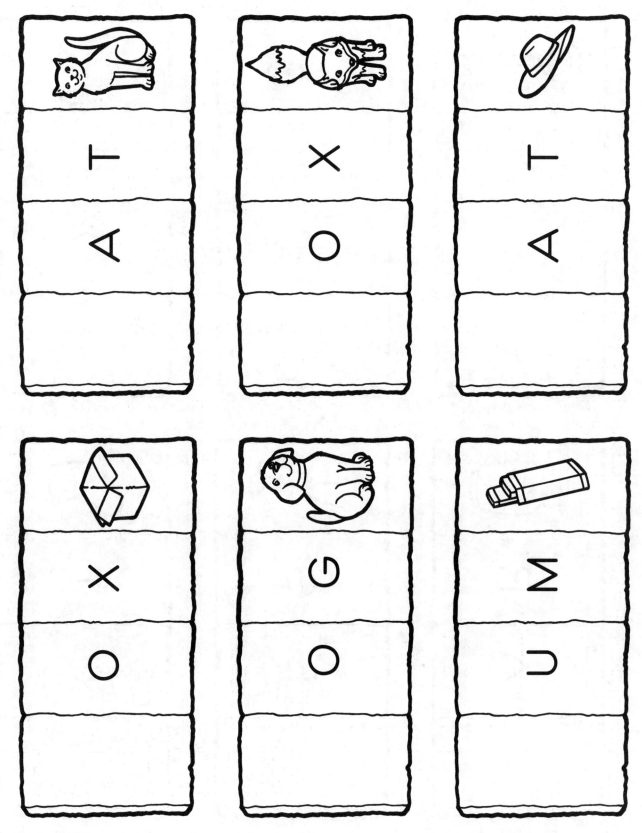

Consonant Crackers *(cont.)*

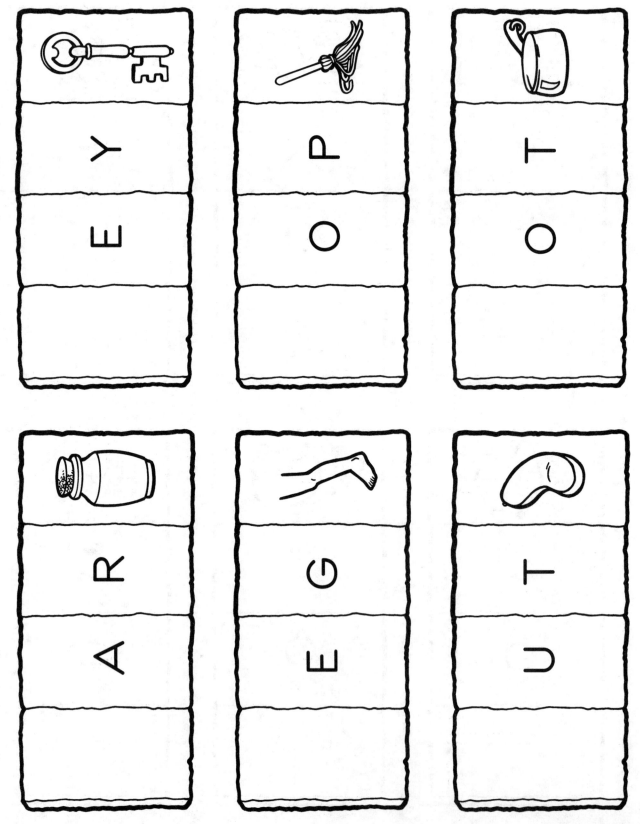

Consonant Crackers (cont.)

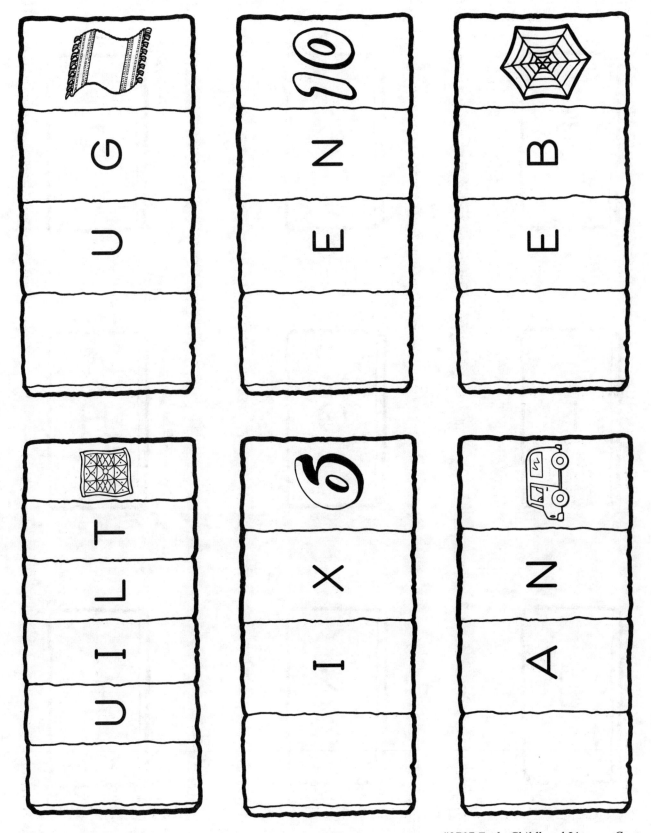

Consonant Crackers *(cont.)*

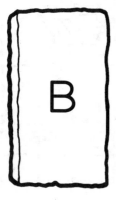

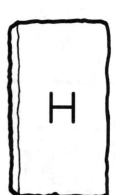

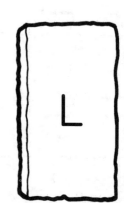

Consonant Crackers *(cont.)*

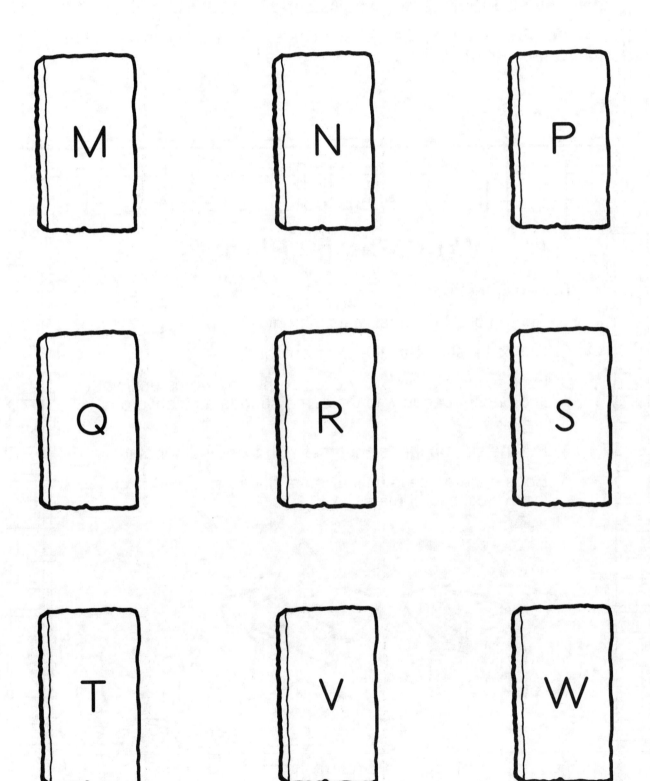

Word Family Planets

Skill: Classifying Words By Word Family

Materials: scissors; planet mats (pages 109–112); stars (page 113)

Teacher Preparation: Cut out star cards. Color and laminate stars and planet mats, if desired.

Word Family Planets

Student Directions

1. Spread out the planet mats in front of you.

2. Choose a star. Say the word out loud.

3. Look at the planets. Say each of the key words until you find one that ends with the same sounds as the word on the star.

4. Put the star on that planet mat. Choose another star.

5. Repeat the process until all stars have been placed on the correct planet mats.

Word Family Planets *(cont.)*

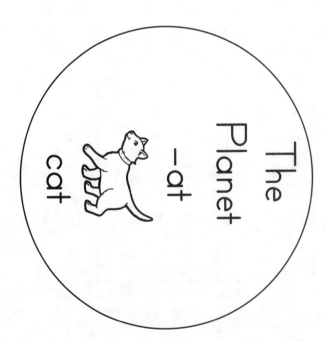

The Planet
-at
cat

Word Family Planets *(cont.)*

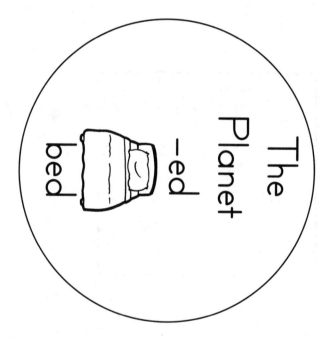

Word Family Planets *(cont.)*

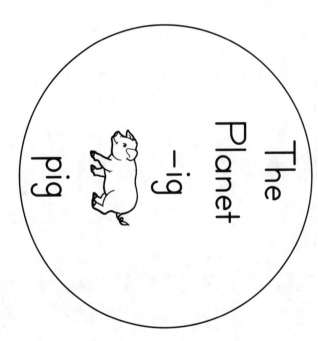

The Planet -ig pig

Word Family Planets *(cont.)*

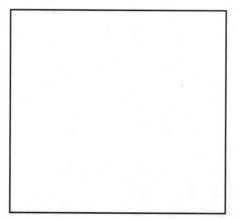

Word Family Planets *(cont.)*

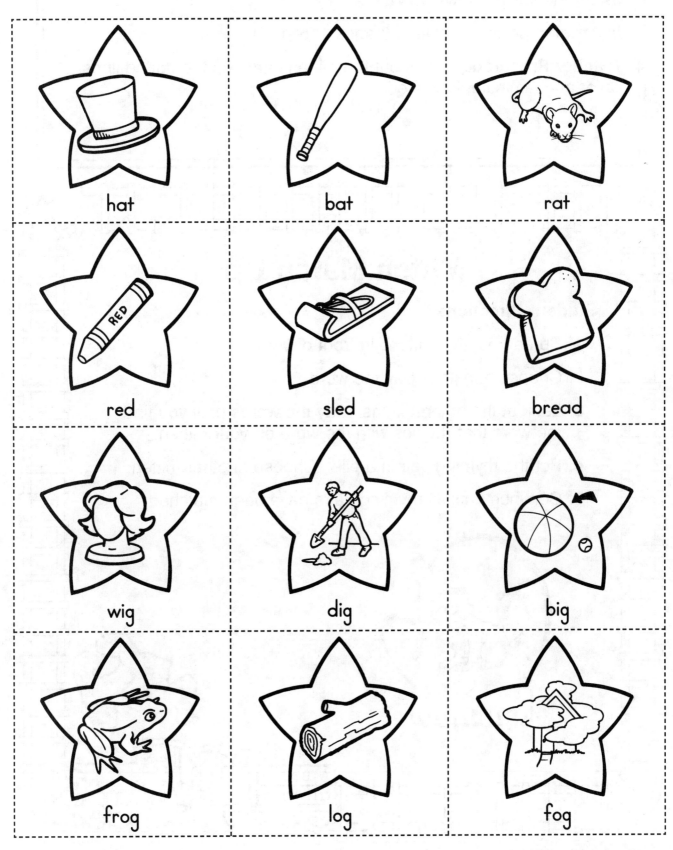

hat

bat

rat

red

sled

bread

wig

dig

big

frog

log

fog

Mitten Match Up

Skill: Identifying Rhyming Words

Materials: scissors; mittens (pages 115–117)

Teacher Preparation: Cut out the mitten cards on the dotted lines. Color and laminate, if desired.

Mitten Match Up

Student Directions

1. Spread out the mittens in front of you.

2. Choose a mitten. Say the word.

3. Look at the other mittens. Say the words until you find the word that rhymes with the word on your mitten.

4. Put the rhyming pair in a pile. Choose another mitten.

5. Continue until all rhyming pairs have been matched.

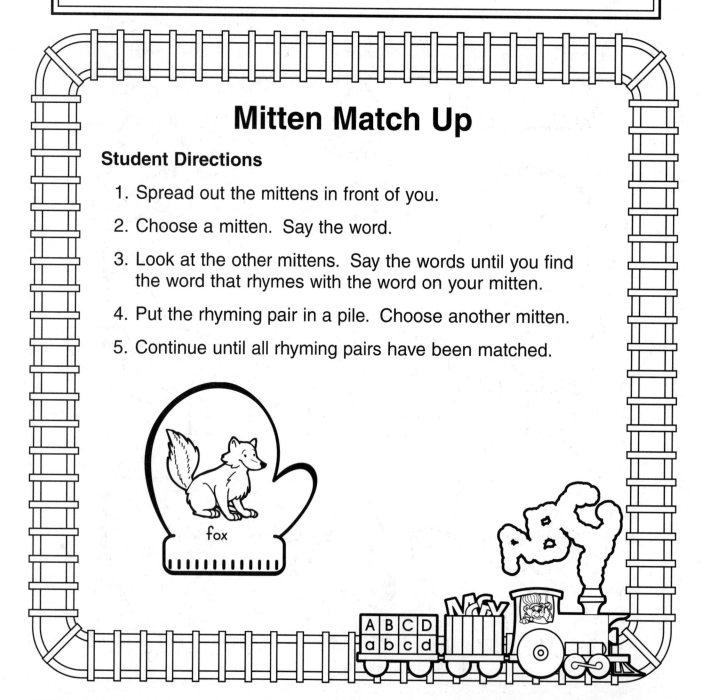

fox

Mitten Match Up *(cont.)*

jar

car

fox

box

lip

zip

Mitten Match Up *(cont.)*

hen

ten

hug

bug

gum

thumb

Mitten Match Up *(cont.)*

mop

top

flag

bag

rock

clock

Word Family Wheels

Skill: Reading Words in Word Families

Materials: selected wheels (pages 119–123); scissors; hole puncher; brass fasteners; pencils

Teacher Preparation: For each center time, you should feature one or two of the word family wheels. (You can use the Word Family Wheels center several times during the year.) Cut out both pieces. Cut out the box on the dotted lines.

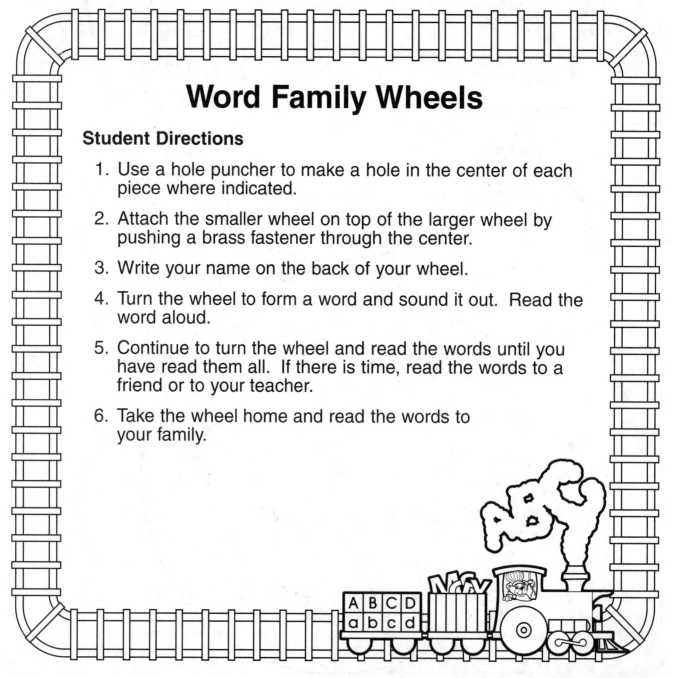

Word Family Wheels

Student Directions

1. Use a hole puncher to make a hole in the center of each piece where indicated.

2. Attach the smaller wheel on top of the larger wheel by pushing a brass fastener through the center.

3. Write your name on the back of your wheel.

4. Turn the wheel to form a word and sound it out. Read the word aloud.

5. Continue to turn the wheel and read the words until you have read them all. If there is time, read the words to a friend or to your teacher.

6. Take the wheel home and read the words to your family.

118

Word Family Wheels *(cont.)*

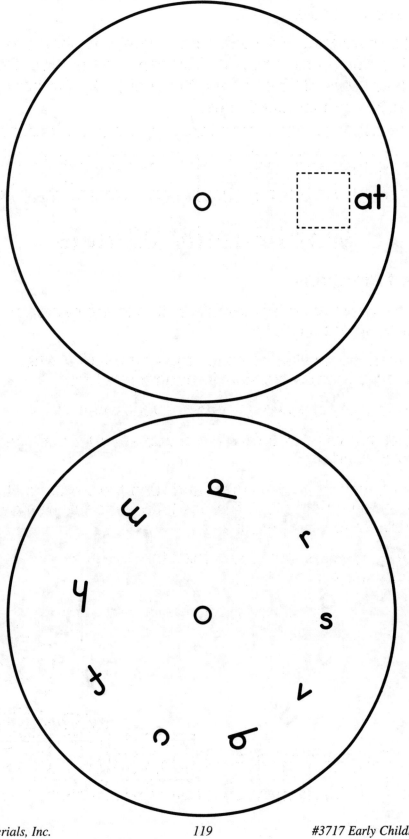

Word Family Wheels *(cont.)*

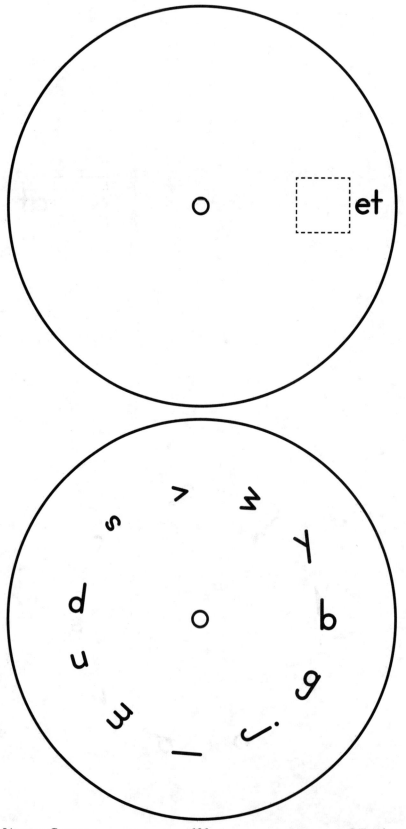

Word Family Wheels *(cont.)*

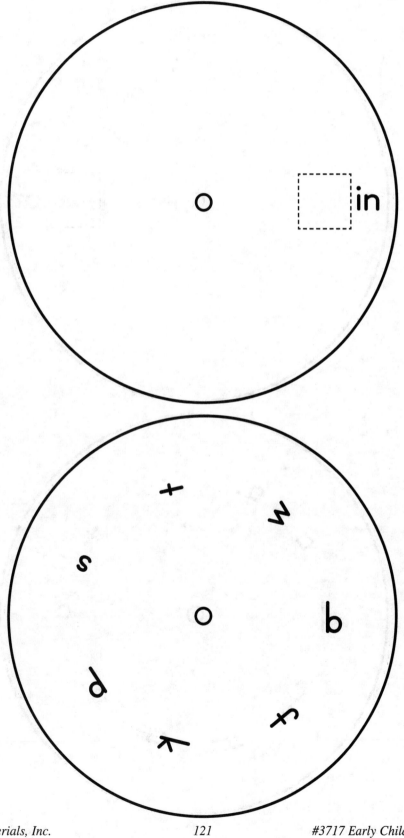

Word Family Wheels *(cont.)*

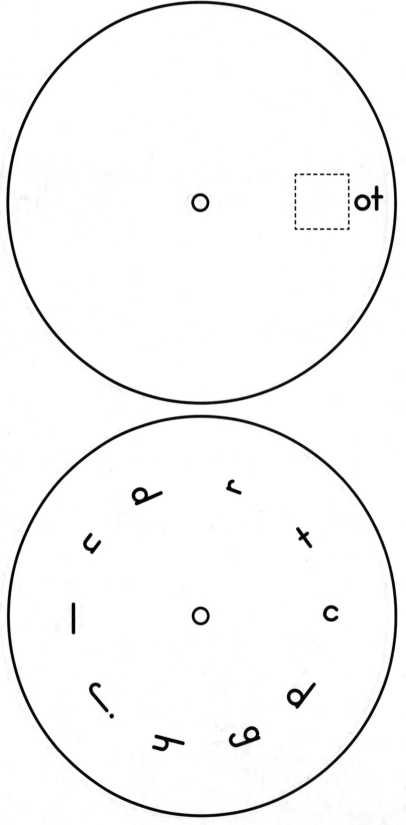

Word Family Wheels *(cont.)*

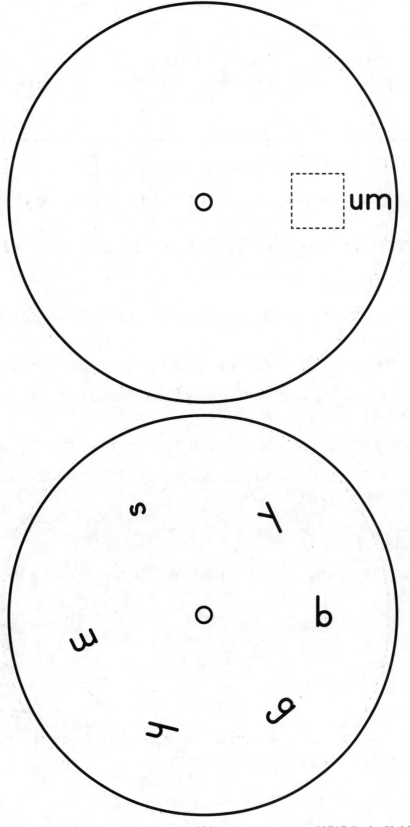

Rhyming Word Concentration

Skill: Identifying Rhyming Words

Materials: scissors; word cards (pages 125–128); number cube Appendix B (page 240)

Teacher Preparation: Cut out and assemble the number cube. Cut out word cards. Color and laminate word cards, if desired.

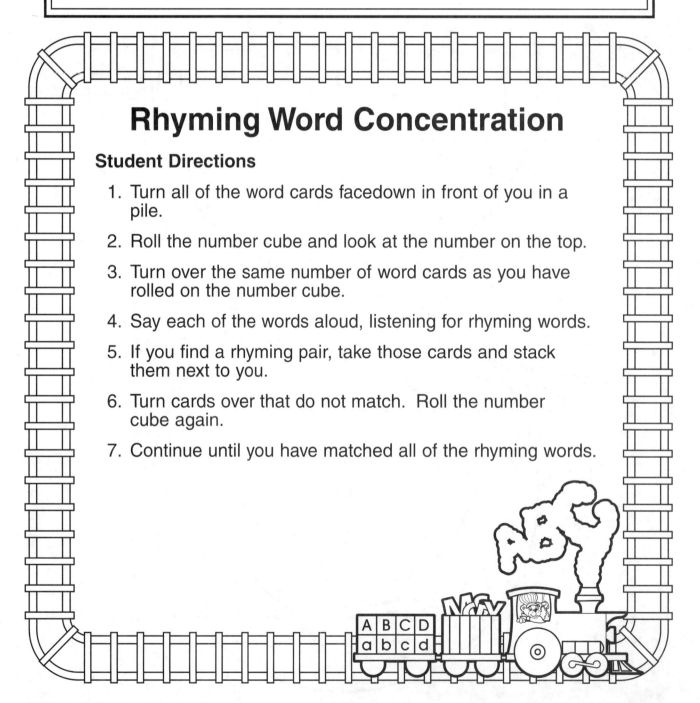

Rhyming Word Concentration

Student Directions

1. Turn all of the word cards facedown in front of you in a pile.

2. Roll the number cube and look at the number on the top.

3. Turn over the same number of word cards as you have rolled on the number cube.

4. Say each of the words aloud, listening for rhyming words.

5. If you find a rhyming pair, take those cards and stack them next to you.

6. Turn cards over that do not match. Roll the number cube again.

7. Continue until you have matched all of the rhyming words.

Rhyming Word Concentration *(cont.)*

cat

bat

ring

swing

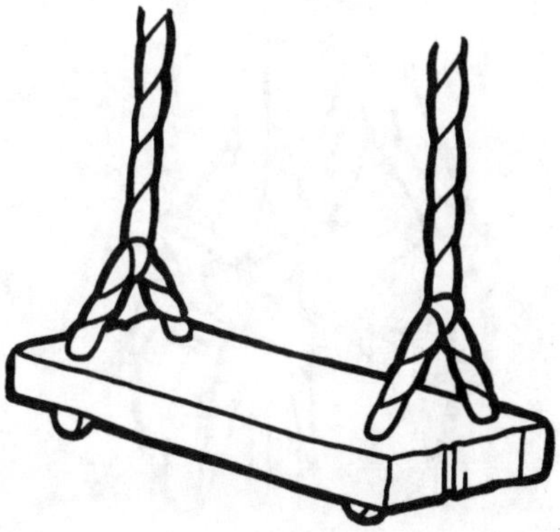

flag

zigzag

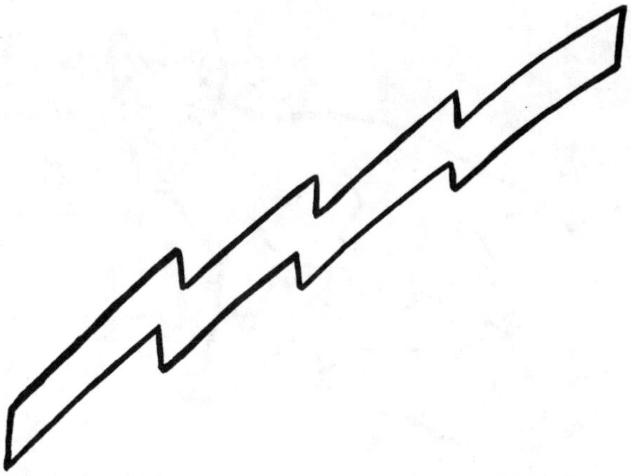

Rhyming Word Concentration *(cont.)*

clock

sock

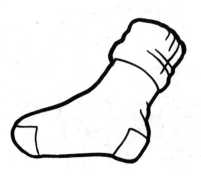

nun

sun

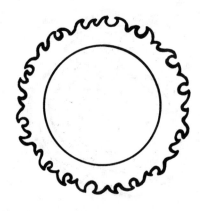

fox

box

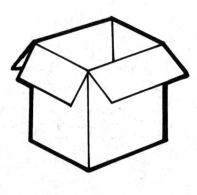

Rhyming Word Concentration *(cont.)*

sled

bread

wig

pig

frog

dog

Rhyming Word Concentration *(cont.)*

hug

bug

gum

thumb

mop

top

Letter Lace-Ups

Skill: Developing Fine Motor Skills, Lacing

Materials: scissors; letters (pages 130–136); hole puncher; yarn or string, knotted on one end.

Teacher Preparation: Cut out letters and punch holes where indicated. Laminate the letters, if possible.

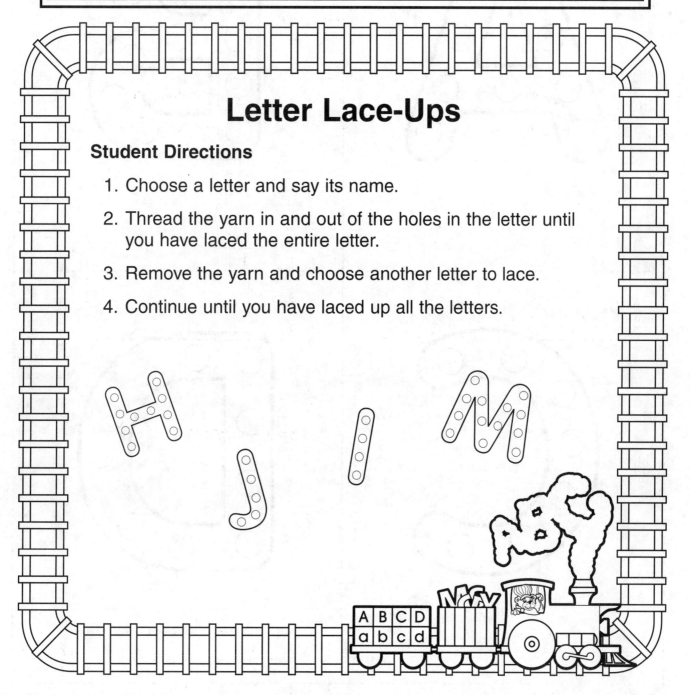

Letter Lace-Ups

Student Directions

1. Choose a letter and say its name.

2. Thread the yarn in and out of the holes in the letter until you have laced the entire letter.

3. Remove the yarn and choose another letter to lace.

4. Continue until you have laced up all the letters.

Letter Lace-Ups *(cont.)*

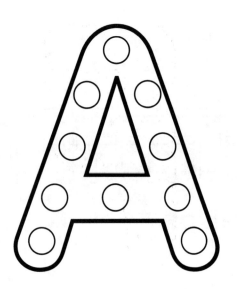

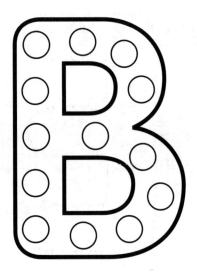

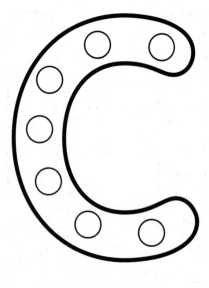

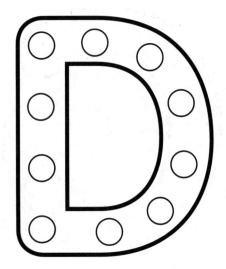

Letter Lace-Ups *(cont.)*

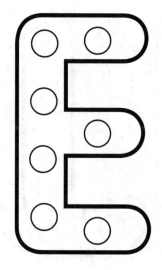

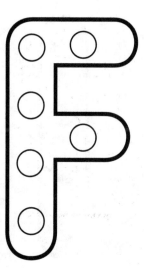

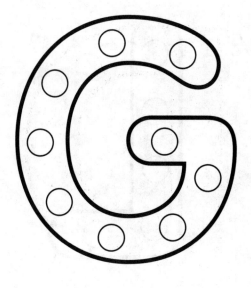

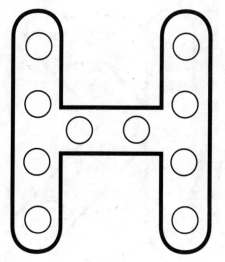

Letter Lace-Ups *(cont.)*

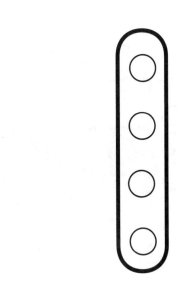

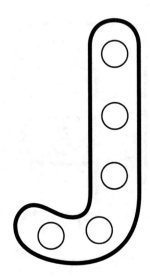

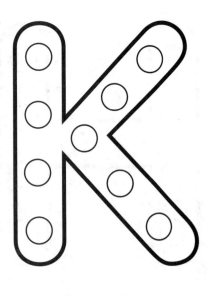

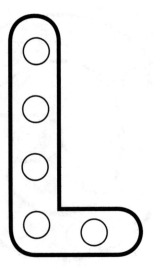

Letter Lace-Ups *(cont.)*

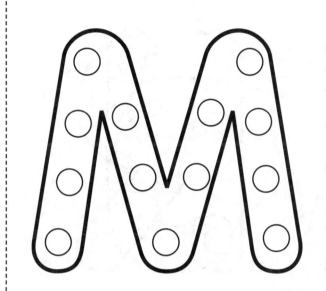

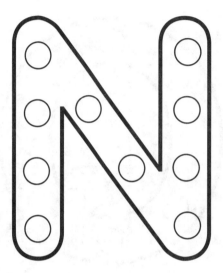

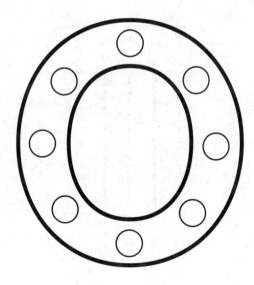

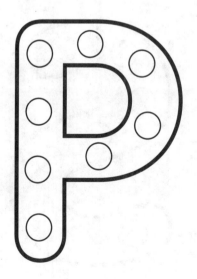

Letter Lace-Ups *(cont.)*

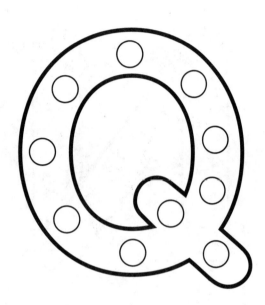

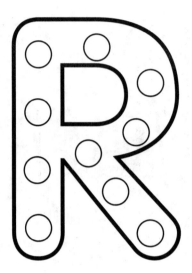

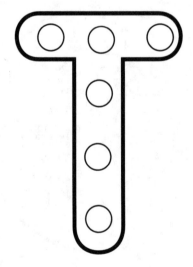

Letter Lace-Ups *(cont.)*

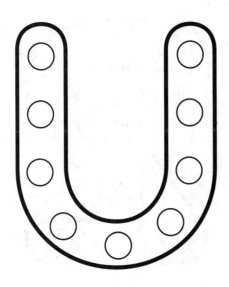
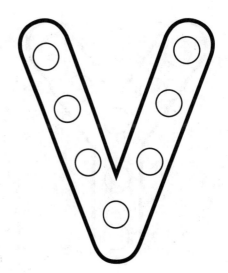
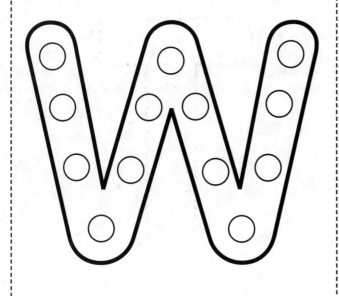
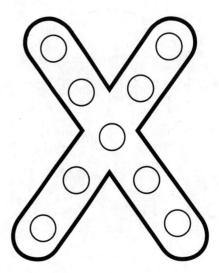

Letter Lace-Ups *(cont.)*

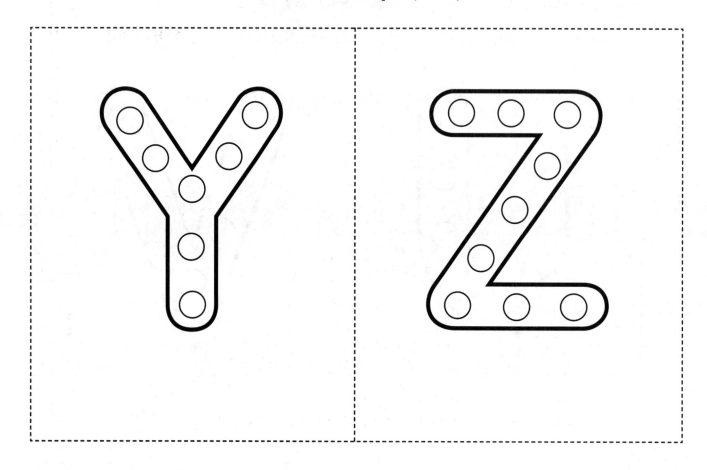

Cut It Out!

Skill: Developing Fine Motor Skills, Cutting

Materials: student copies of the cutting patterns (pages 138–139); scissors; pencils

Teacher Preparation: Reproduce cutting patterns (pages 138-139) for each student in your class.

Cut It Out!

Student Directions

1. Choose a cutting pattern and write your name on the line at the top of the page.

2. Find the star at the edge of the paper. Use your scissors to carefully cut along the dotted line until you reach the picture at the end.

3. Continue until you have cut all the lines on the page.

4. Choose another cutting pattern page and repeat the process until you have cut all of the lines.

Cut It Out! *(cont.)*

Name

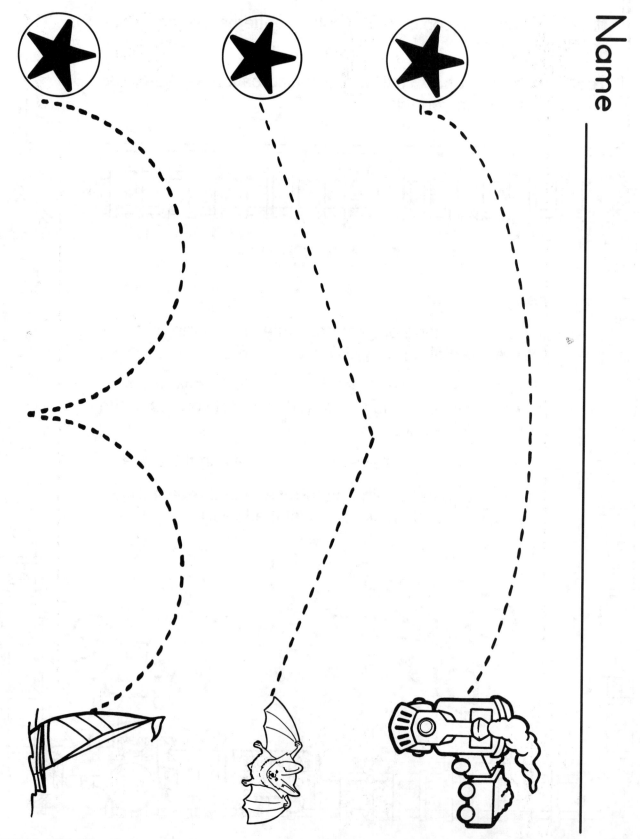

Cut It Out! *(cont.)*

Name

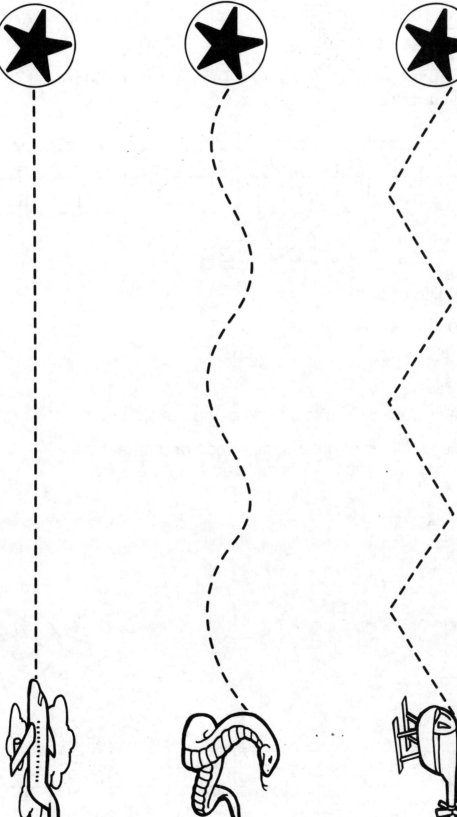

Good Eggs

Skill: Developing Fine Motor Skills, Writing

Materials: student copies of eggs (pages 141–143); pencils; crayons or markers

Teacher Preparation: Copy the eggs (pages 141-143) for each student in your class.

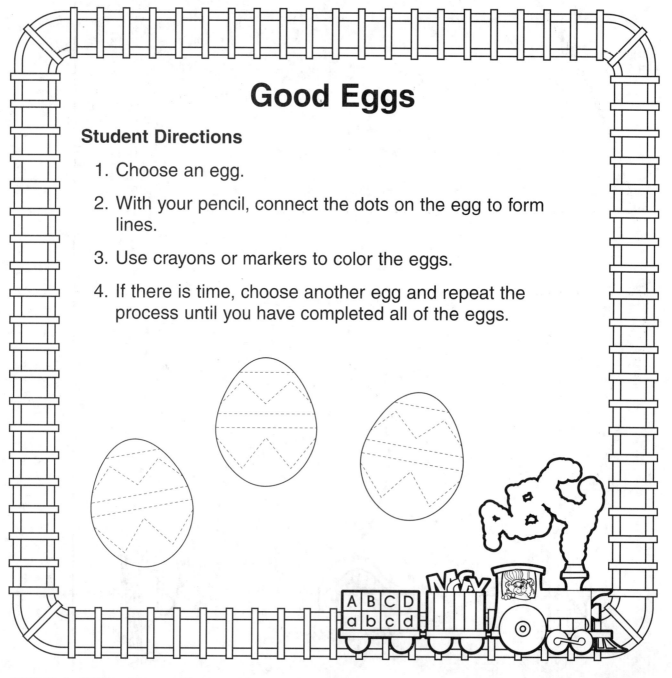

Good Eggs

Student Directions

1. Choose an egg.

2. With your pencil, connect the dots on the egg to form lines.

3. Use crayons or markers to color the eggs.

4. If there is time, choose another egg and repeat the process until you have completed all of the eggs.

Good Eggs *(cont.)*

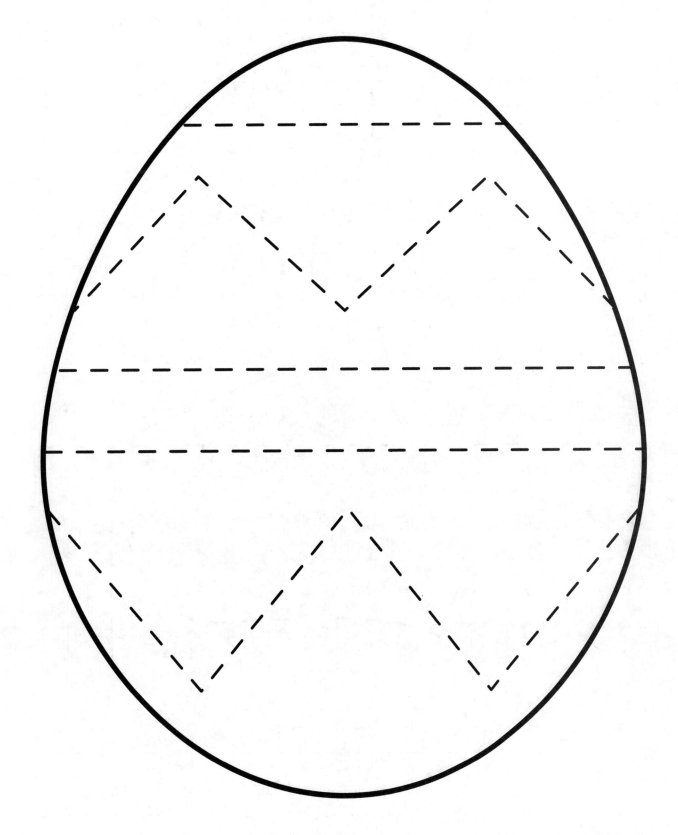

Good Eggs *(cont.)*

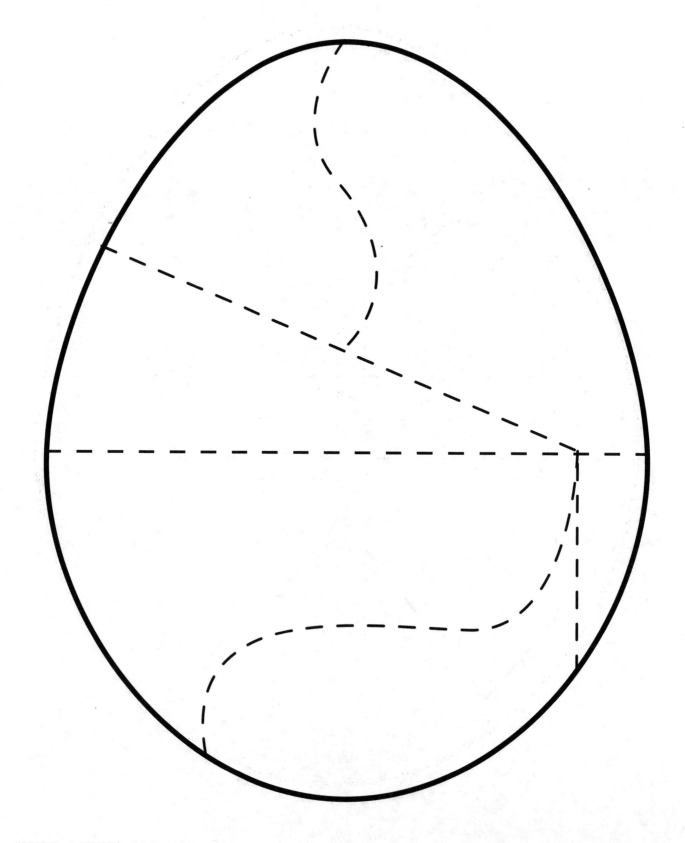

Good Eggs *(cont.)*

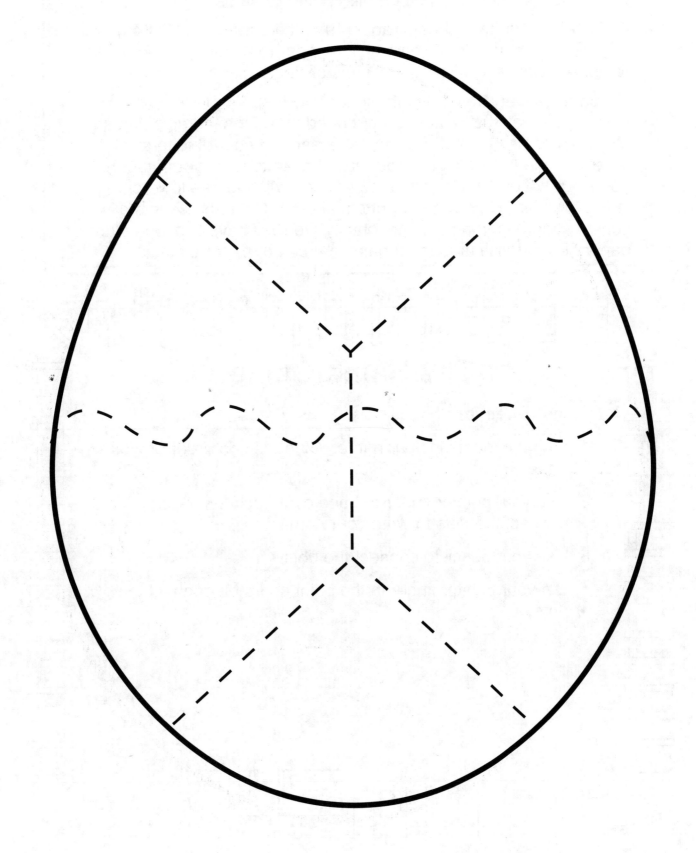

The Name Game

Skill: Developing Fine Motor Skills, Writing Names

Materials: letter tally sheet (page 149); letters (pages 145–149); scissors; large sheets of construction paper (any color); pencils; glue; tempera paint (any color); small cups or paper plates

Teacher Preparation: Use the letter tally sheet to determine how many copies of each letter you will need in order to complete each student's name. Reproduce the necessary number of letters. Cut the letters on the dotted lines. (You may choose to write your students' names in dotted letters on the paper if you wish to use lowercase letters or omit the copying of dotted letters.) Cut large sheets of construction paper in half, horizontally. You will have two long strips of paper. Put a small amount of paint in a cup or paper plate.

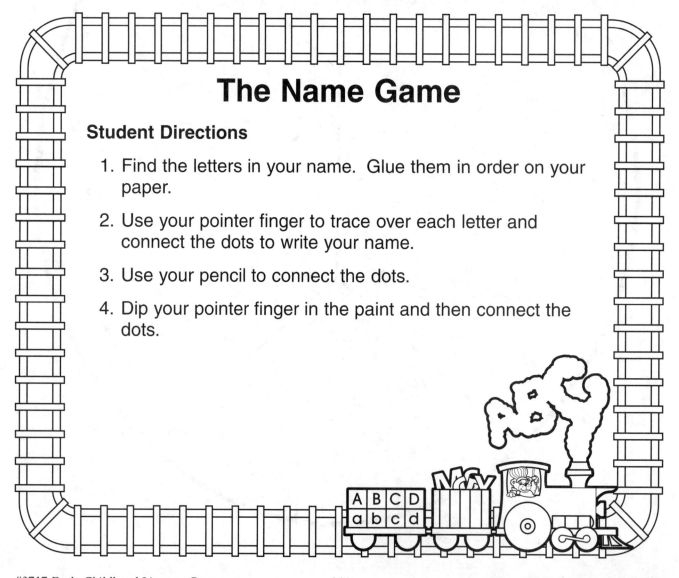

The Name Game

Student Directions

1. Find the letters in your name. Glue them in order on your paper.

2. Use your pointer finger to trace over each letter and connect the dots to write your name.

3. Use your pencil to connect the dots.

4. Dip your pointer finger in the paint and then connect the dots.

The Name Game *(cont.)*

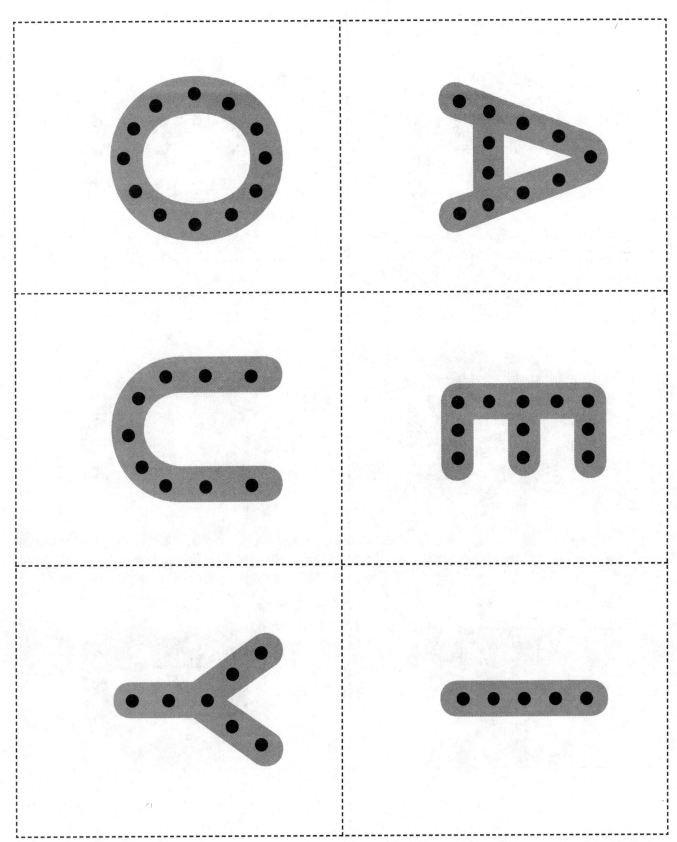

The Name Game *(cont.)*

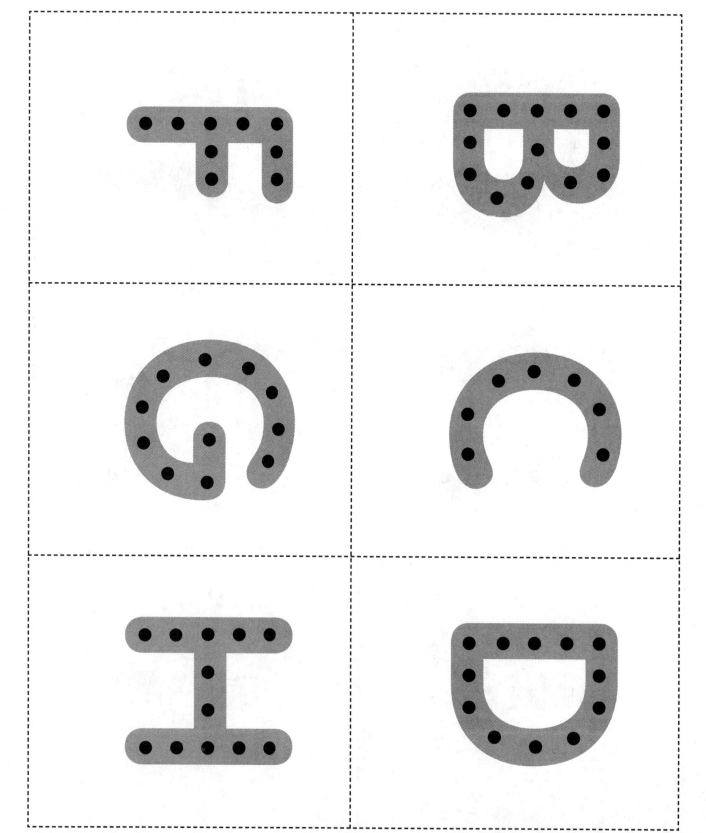

The Name Game *(cont.)*

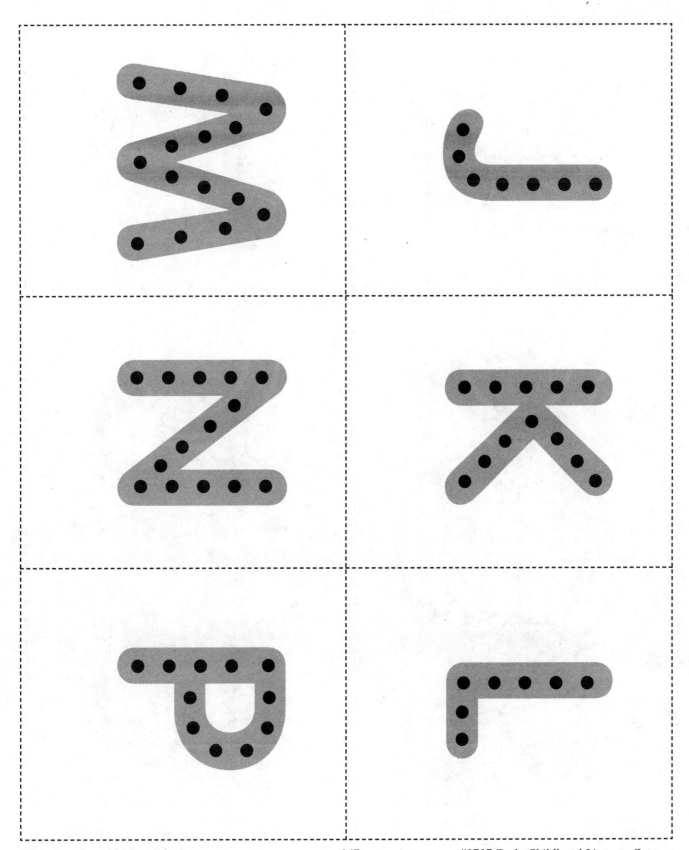

The Name Game *(cont.)*

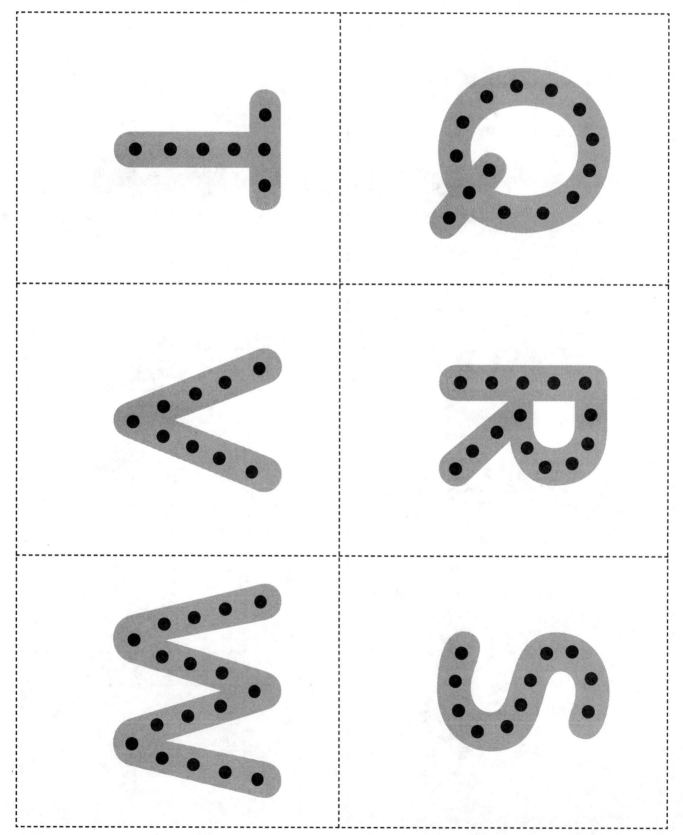

The Name Game *(cont.)*

Letter Tally Sheet

A		L	
E		M	
I		N	
O		P	
U		Q	
Y		R	
B		S	
C		T	
D		V	
F		W	
G		X	
H		Y	
J		Z	
K			

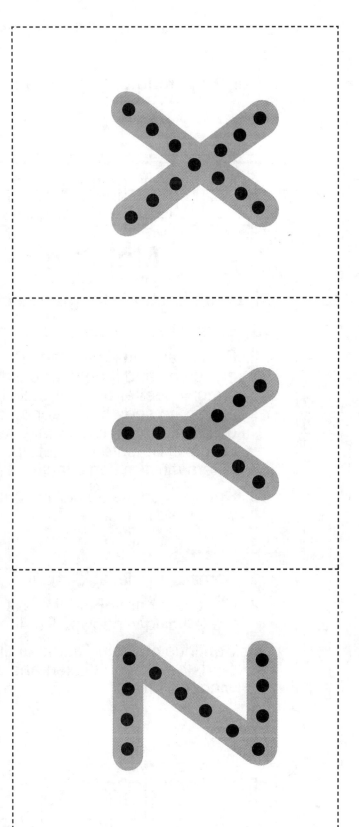

Matching Windows

Skill: Visual Discrimination

Materials: scissors; buildings (pages 151–154); cards (pages 155–156)

Teacher Preparation: Cut out cards. Laminate cards and buildings, if desired.

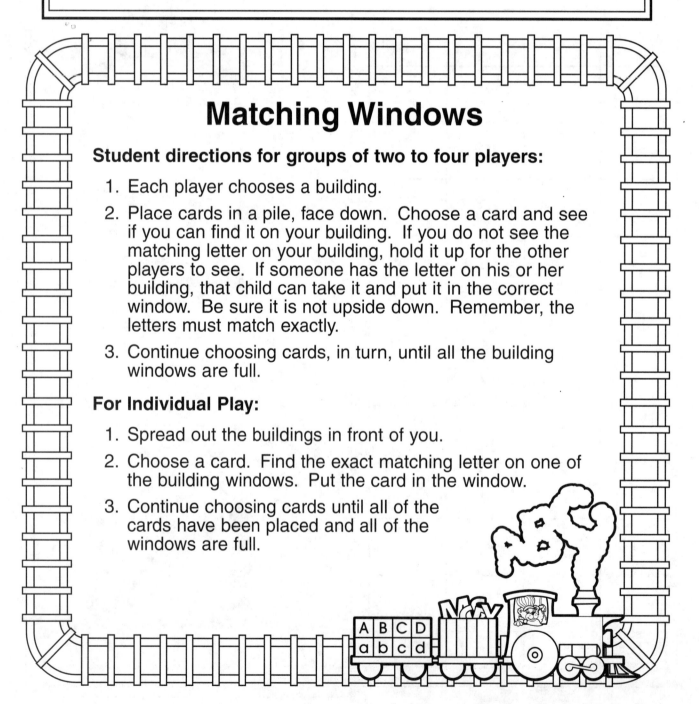

Matching Windows

Student directions for groups of two to four players:

1. Each player chooses a building.

2. Place cards in a pile, face down. Choose a card and see if you can find it on your building. If you do not see the matching letter on your building, hold it up for the other players to see. If someone has the letter on his or her building, that child can take it and put it in the correct window. Be sure it is not upside down. Remember, the letters must match exactly.

3. Continue choosing cards, in turn, until all the building windows are full.

For Individual Play:

1. Spread out the buildings in front of you.

2. Choose a card. Find the exact matching letter on one of the building windows. Put the card in the window.

3. Continue choosing cards until all of the cards have been placed and all of the windows are full.

Matching Windows *(cont.)*

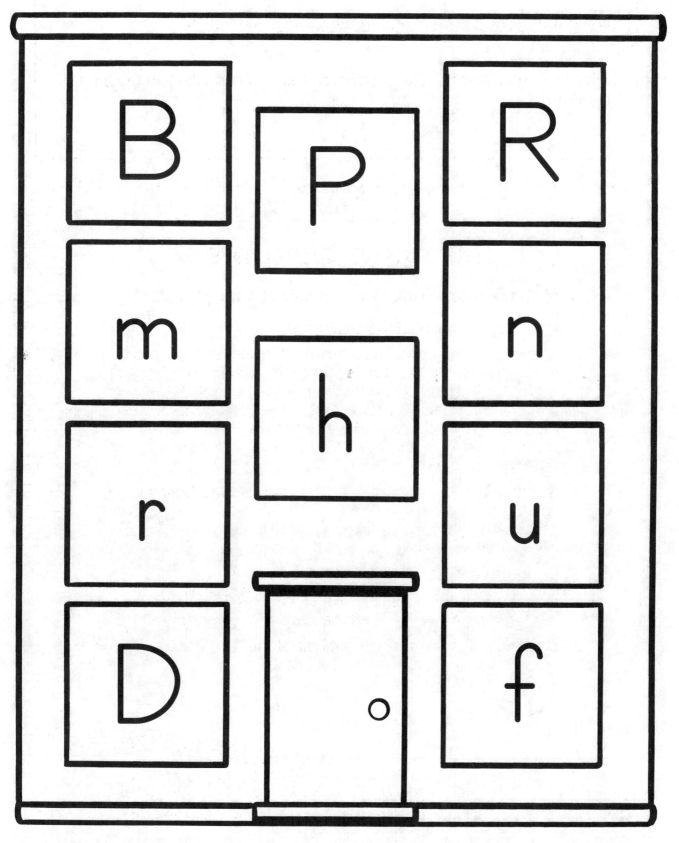

Matching Windows *(cont.)*

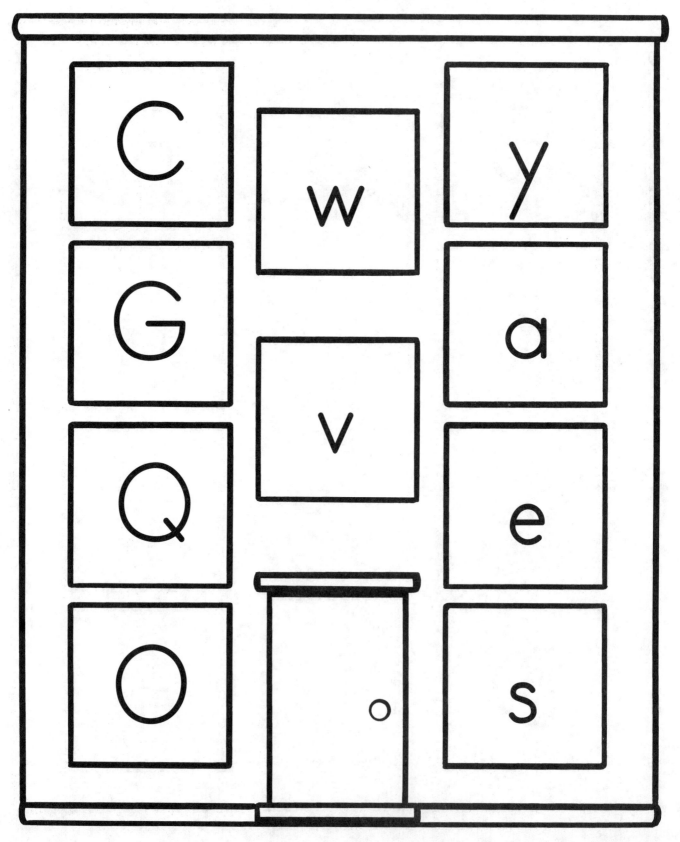

Matching Windows *(cont.)*

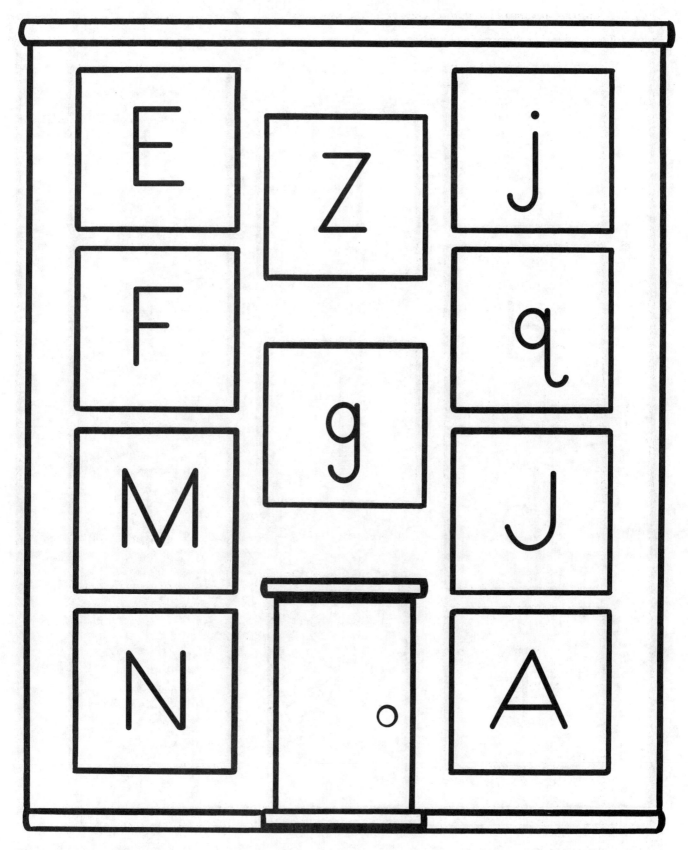

Matching Windows *(cont.)*

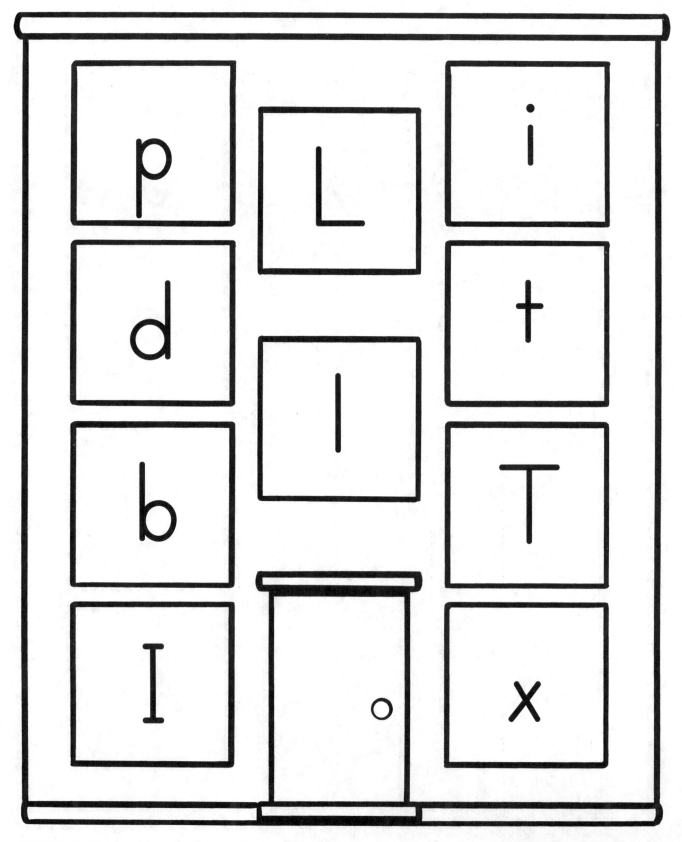

154

Matching Windows *(cont.)*

r	g	q	j
T	t	w	v
u	y	a	Z
e	h	J	A
s	D	f	x

Matching Windows *(cont.)*

p	d	b	B
R	P	E	F
C	G	Q	O
I	L	l	i
M	N	m	n

Lock and Key

Skill: Visual Discrimination

Materials: scissors; locks (pages 158–160); keys (page 161)

Teacher Preparation: reproduce cutting patterns (pages 138-139) for each student in your class.

Lock and Key

Student Directions

1. Lay out the keys in front of you.

2. Choose a lock. Look for the key with the identical design on it. Be sure to look at the size and shape of the design to be sure it matches exactly.

3. Put the matching key on the lock.

4. Continue until all of the locks have been matched with the correct key.

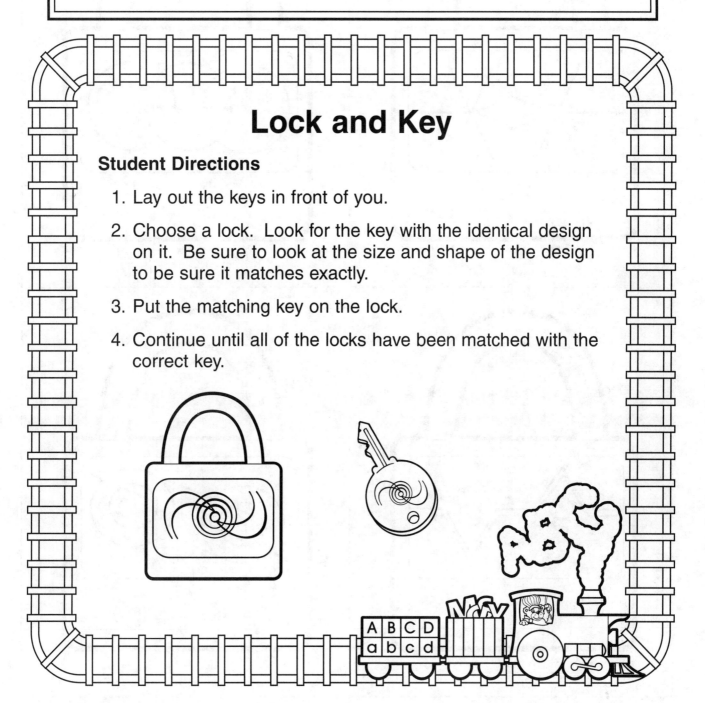

Lock and Key *(cont.)*

158

Lock and Key *(cont.)*

Lock and Key *(cont.)*

160

Lock and Key *(cont.)*

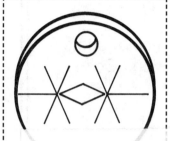

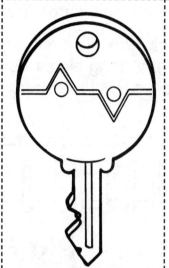

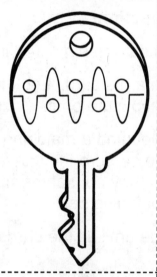

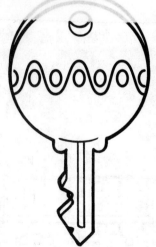

Pig Poses

Skill: Visual Discrimination

Materials: scissors; pig cards (pages 163–166); pencil

Teacher Preparation: Cut out pig cards. Put matching color spots on the back of matching pig cards for student self-checking. Color and laminate pig cards, if desired.

Pig Poses

Student Directions

1. Spread out the pig cards in front of you.

2. Choose a pig card. Look for another card that has an identical picture on it.

3. When you find a matching set, turn the cards over and check to be sure they have the same marking on the back. If they do, set them aside. If they do not, they are not a matching set.

4. Continue until all the cards have been matched.

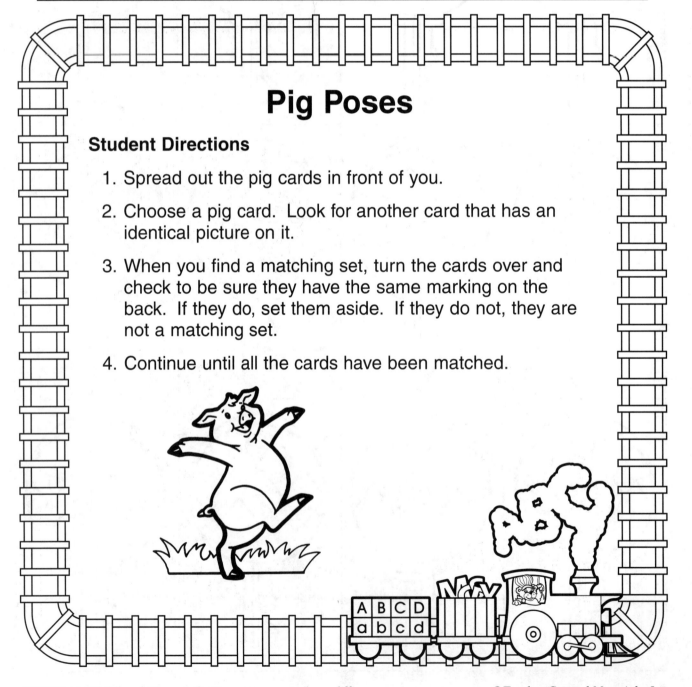

Pig Poses *(cont.)*

Pig Poses (cont.)

164

Pig Poses *(cont.)*

Pig Poses *(cont.)*

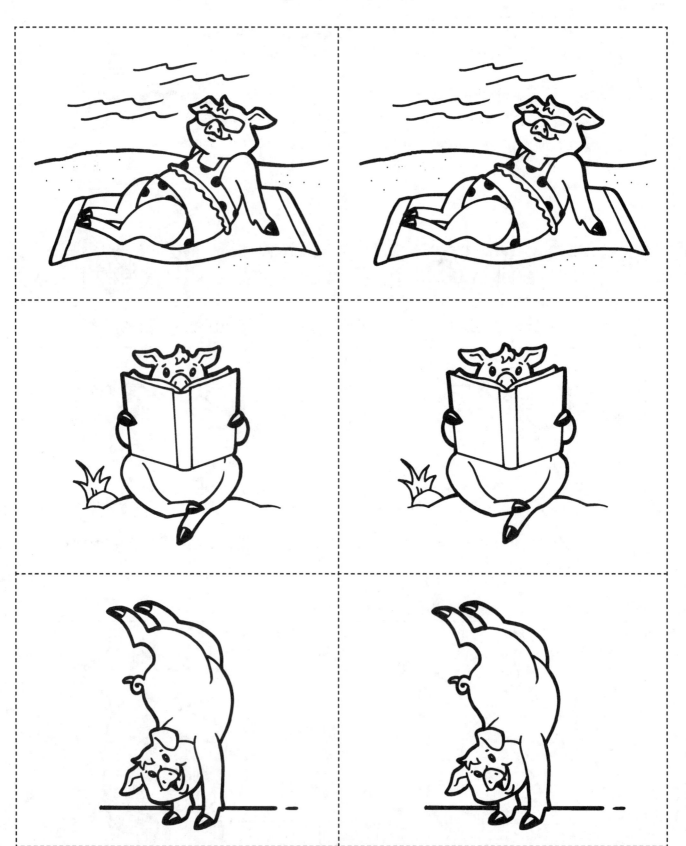

"Egg-Cellent" Vowels

Skill: Identifying Long Vowel Sounds

Materials: scissors; eggs and cartons (pages 168–172); pencil

Teacher Preparation: Cut out eggs and cartons. Write the correct vowel on the back of each egg for student self-checking. Color and laminate eggs and cartons, if desired.

"Egg-Cellent" Vowels

Student Directions

1. Spread out the cartons in front of you.

2. Choose one egg. Say the word aloud, listening to the beginning sound.

3. Determine which carton the egg goes into. (Remember, a long vowel says its name.)

4. Put the egg in the correct carton and choose another egg.

5. Continue until all the eggs are in the correct cartons.

6. Check your work by looking on the back of each egg to see if the vowel is the same as the one on the carton.

"Egg-Cellent" Vowels *(cont.)*

$\overline{\text{A}}$ $\overline{\text{a}}$

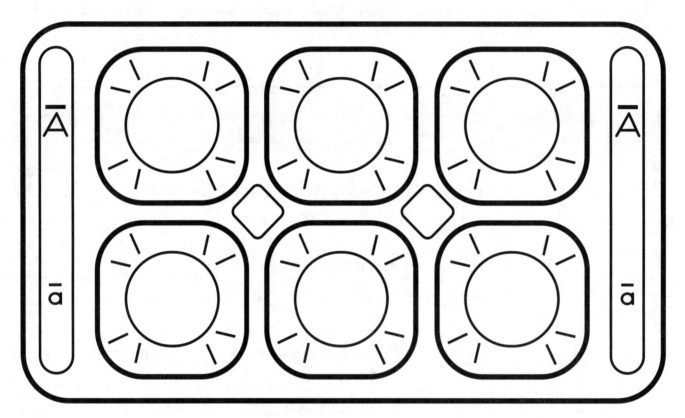

acorn

angel

ape

ankle

anchor

apron

168 ©Teacher Created Materials, Inc.

"Egg-Cellent" Vowels *(cont.)*

Ē ē

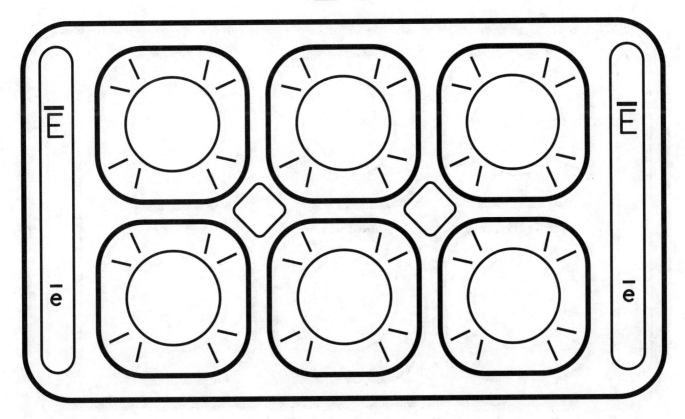

eagle

easel

eel

eleven

eraser

Easter

"Egg-Cellent" Vowels *(cont.)*

Ī ĭ

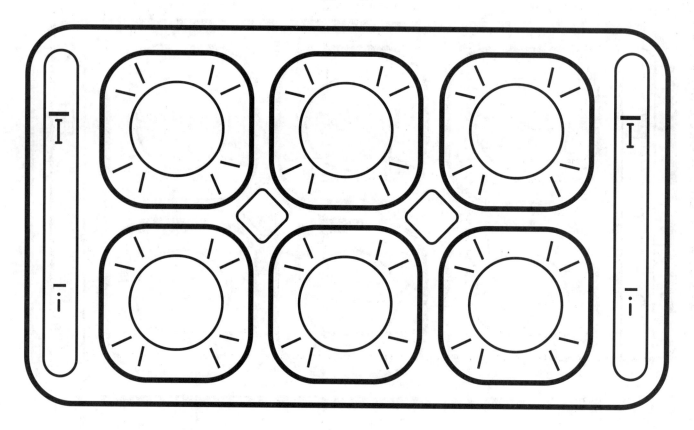

ice

ice cream

icicle

iron

ice skater

island

"Egg-Cellent" Vowels *(cont.)*

Ō ŏ

oatmeal

ocean

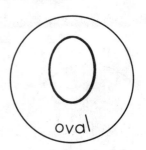
oval

overalls

over

open

"Egg-Cellent" Vowels *(cont.)*

Ū ū

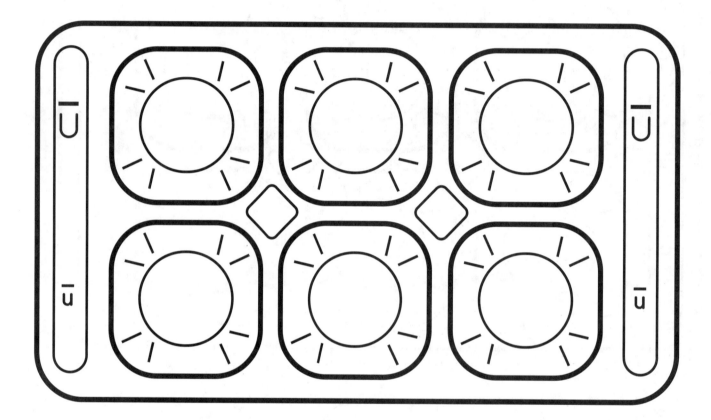

uniform

unicorn

United States

ukelele

unicycle

utensils

172

Pizza Party

Skill: Identifying Short Vowel Sounds.

Materials: scissors; pizza and pepperoni reproducibles (pages 174–178); pencil

Teacher Preparation: Cut out pizza slices and pepperoni. Write the correct vowel on the back of each pepperoni slice for student self-checking. Color and laminate pizza and pepperoni, if desired.

Pizza Party

Student Directions

1. Spread out the pizza slices in front of you. Review each short vowel sound.

2. Choose a pepperoni slice. Say the word aloud, listening for the beginning sound.

3. Place the pepperoni slice on the correct pizza slice.

4. Continue until all pepperoni slices are on the correct pizza slices.

5. Check your work by looking at the letter on the back of each pepperoni slice to see if it matches the letter on the pizza slice you have chosen.

Pizza Party *(cont.)*

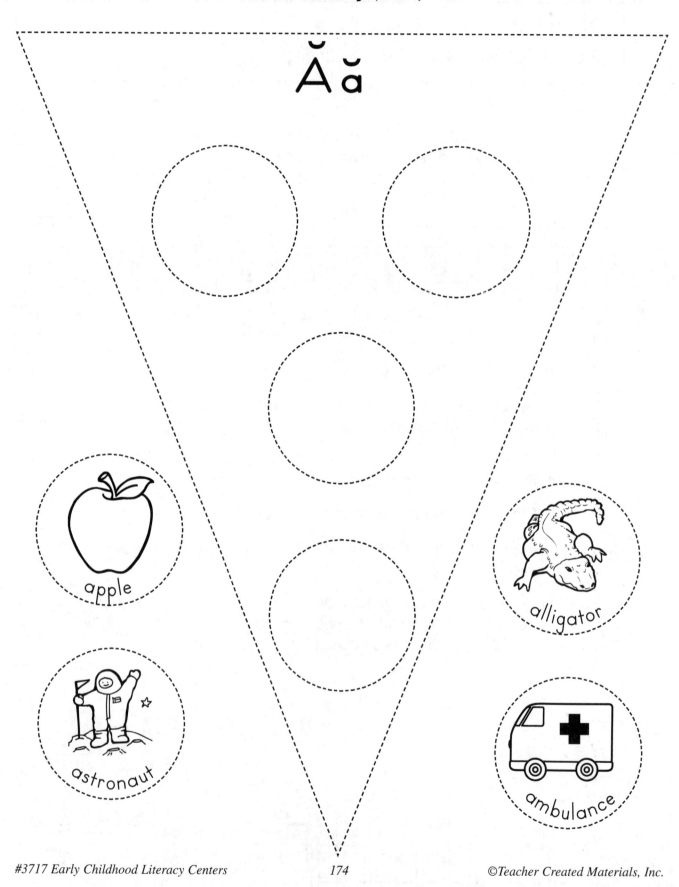

apple

alligator

astronaut

ambulance

Pizza Party *(cont.)*

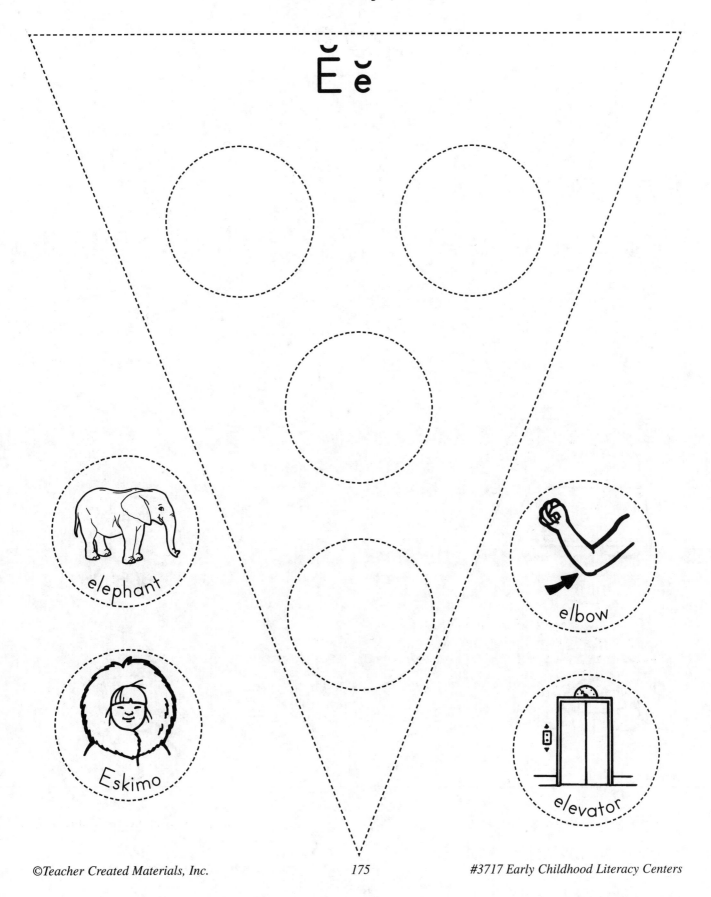

Ĕ ĕ

elephant

elbow

Eskimo

elevator

Pizza Party *(cont.)*

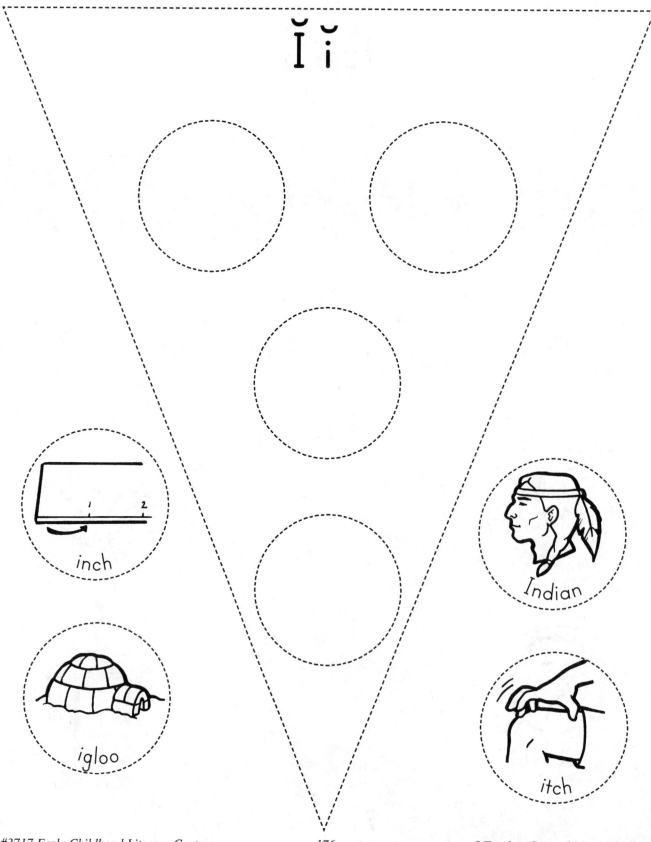

Ĭ ĭ

inch

igloo

Indian

itch

Pizza Party *(cont.)*

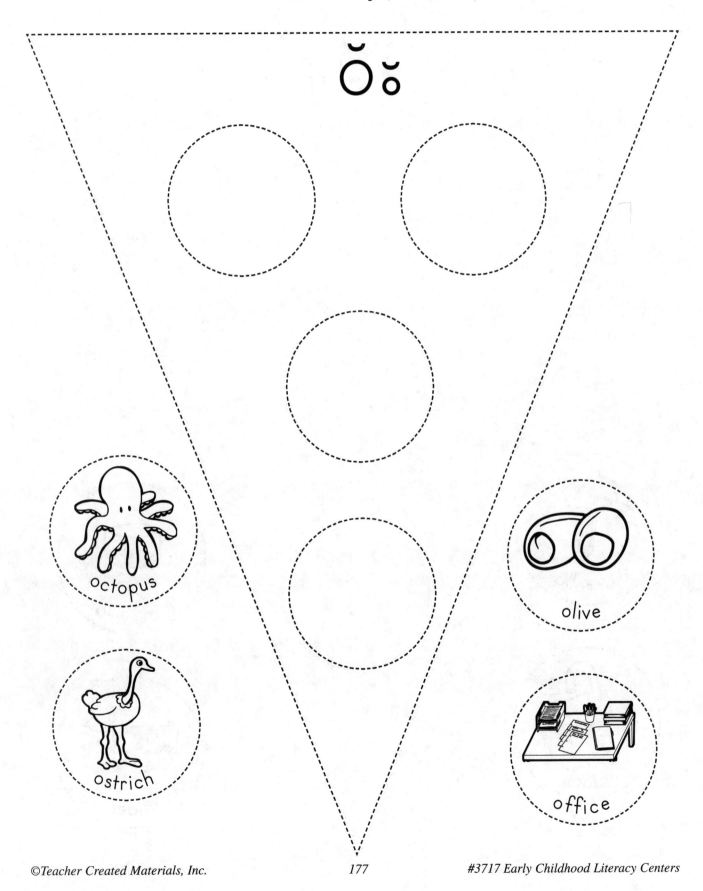

Pizza Party *(cont.)*

Ŭ ŭ

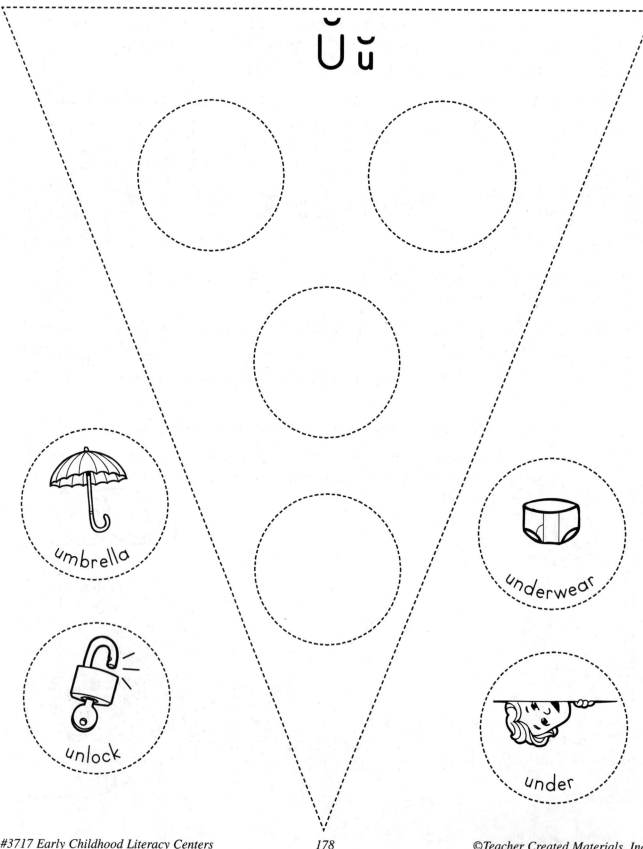

umbrella

underwear

unlock

under

By the Book

Skill: Distinguishing Between Long and Short Vowel Sounds

Materials: scissors; books (pages 180–184); pictures (pages 185–187); pencil

Teacher Preparation: Cut out the pictures. Write the correct long or short vowel on the back of each picture for student self-checking. Color and laminate pictures and books, if desired.

By the Book

Student Directions

1. Spread out the books in front of you. Review each long- and short-vowel sound.

2. Choose a picture. Say the word aloud, listening for the beginning sound.

3. Place the picture on the correct book page by matching the beginning sound.

4. Continue until all pictures are on the correct book pages.

5. Check your work by looking at the vowel written on the back of each picture. It should match the vowel on the page you chose.

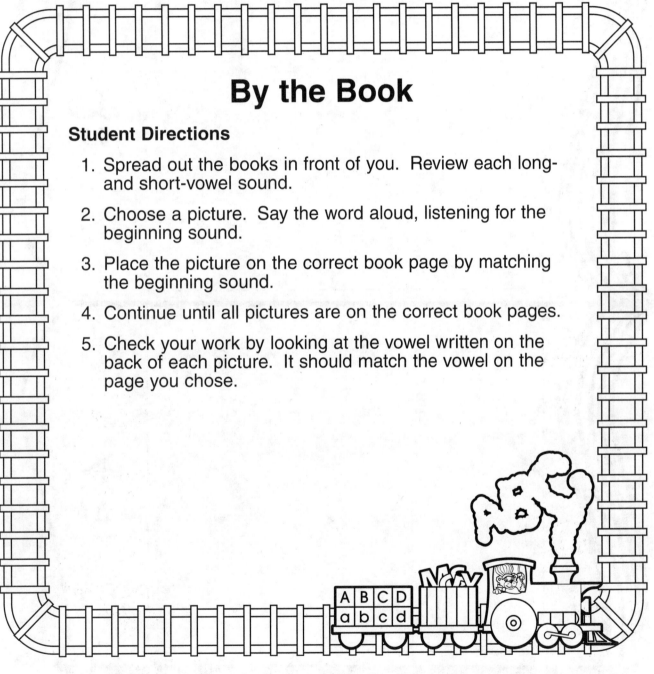

By the Book *(cont.)*

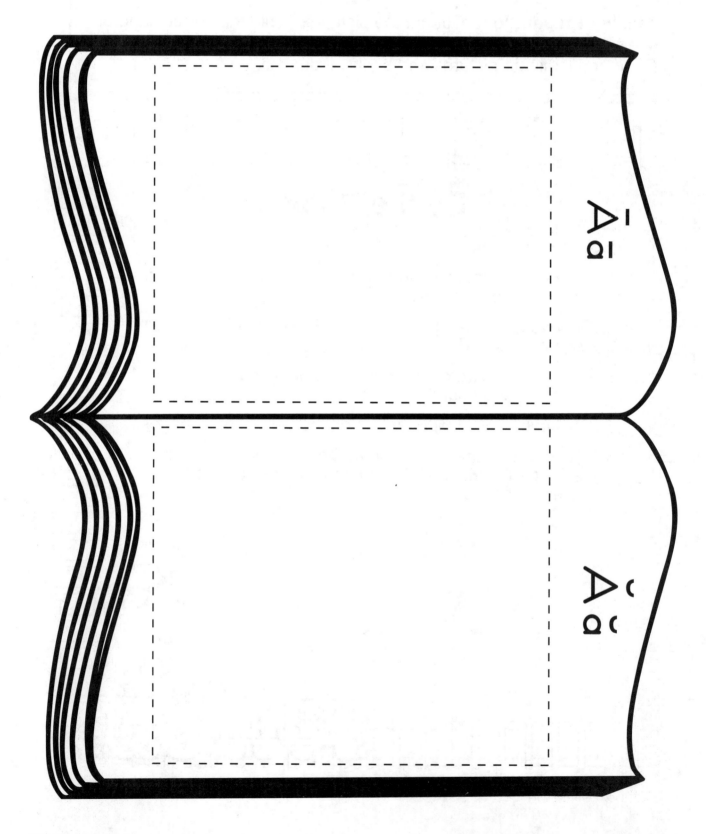

By the Book *(cont.)*

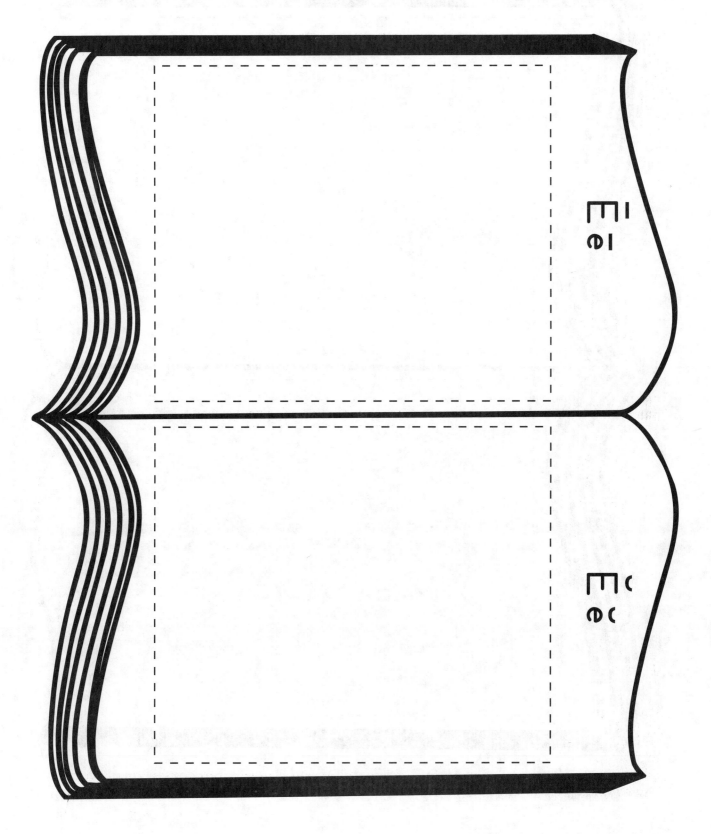

By the Book *(cont.)*

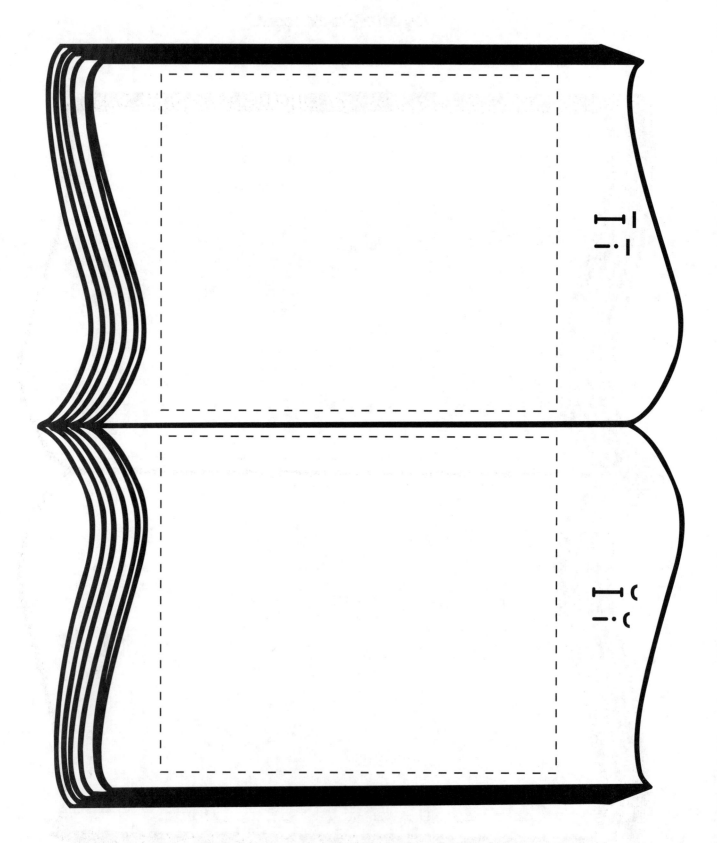

By the Book *(cont.)*

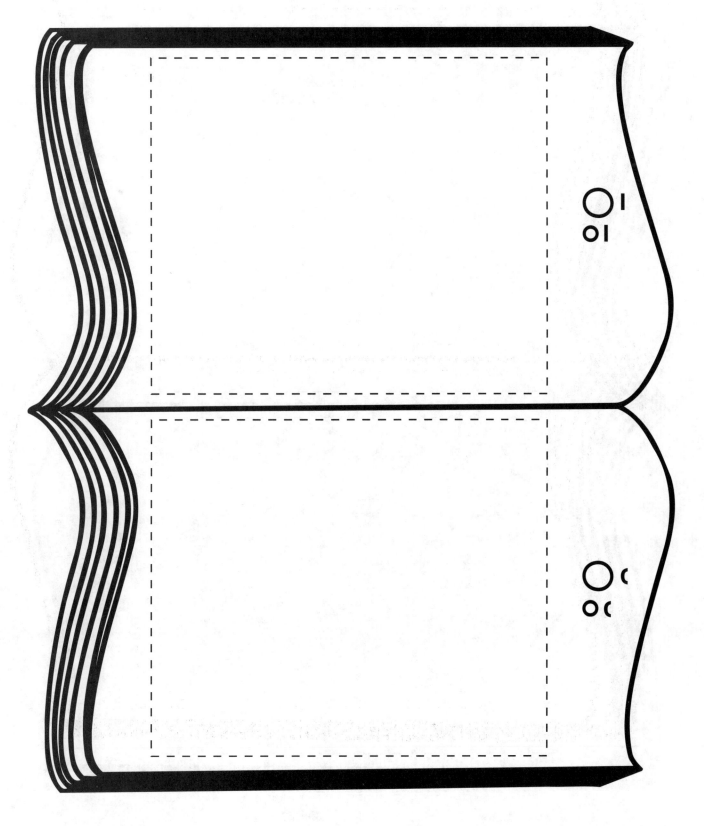

By the Book *(cont.)*

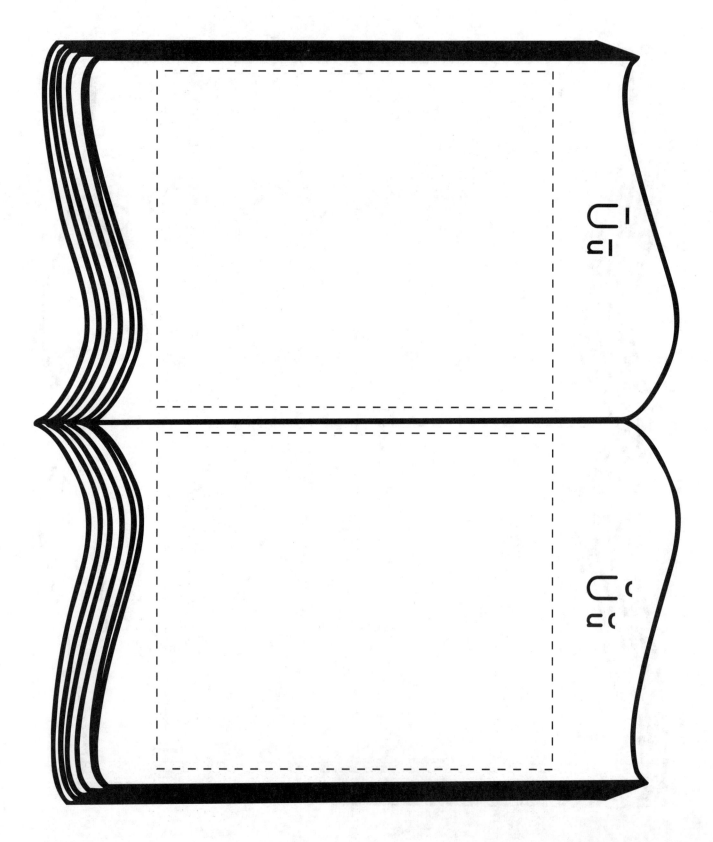

By the Book *(cont.)*

acorn

apple

eagle

elephant

By the Book *(cont.)*

ice cream

igloo

oval

octopus

By the Book *(cont.)*

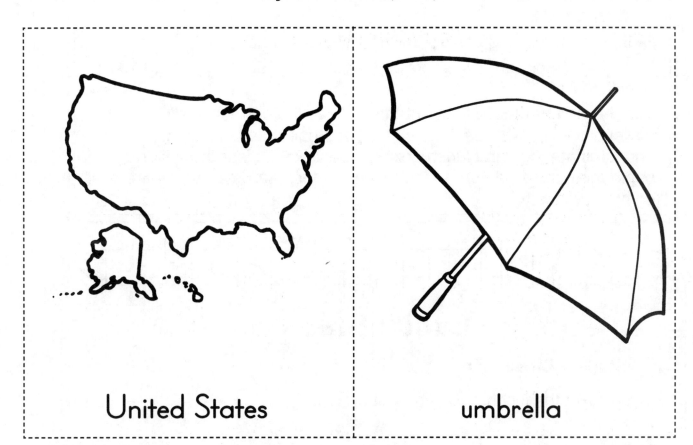

United States   umbrella

Lunch Break

Skill: Distinguishing Long and Short Vowel Sounds

Materials: scissors; lunch boxes (pages 189–190); food (page 191); pencil

Teacher Preparation: Cut out food. Write the correct long or short vowel on the back of each food card for student self-checking. Color and laminate food and lunch boxes, if desired. Before the children begin the center, be sure to introduce the food cards as some are not common foods.

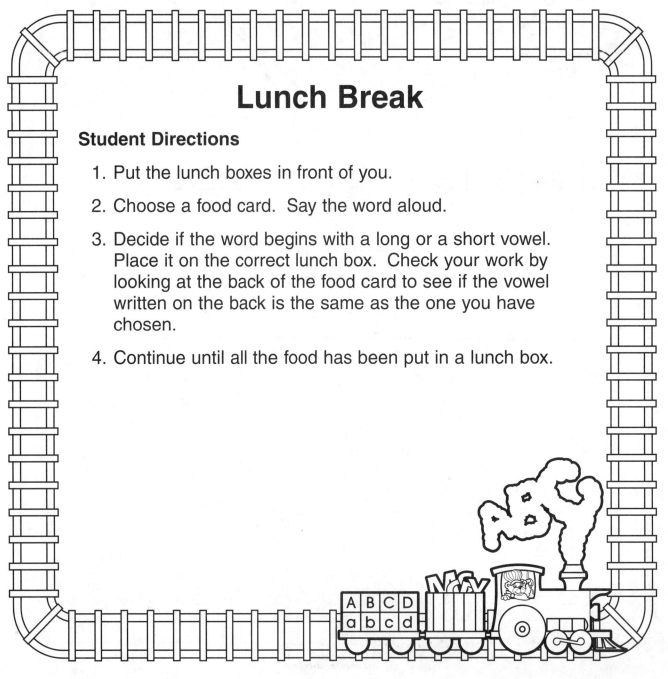

Lunch Break

Student Directions

1. Put the lunch boxes in front of you.

2. Choose a food card. Say the word aloud.

3. Decide if the word begins with a long or a short vowel. Place it on the correct lunch box. Check your work by looking at the back of the food card to see if the vowel written on the back is the same as the one you have chosen.

4. Continue until all the food has been put in a lunch box.

Lunch Break *(cont.)*

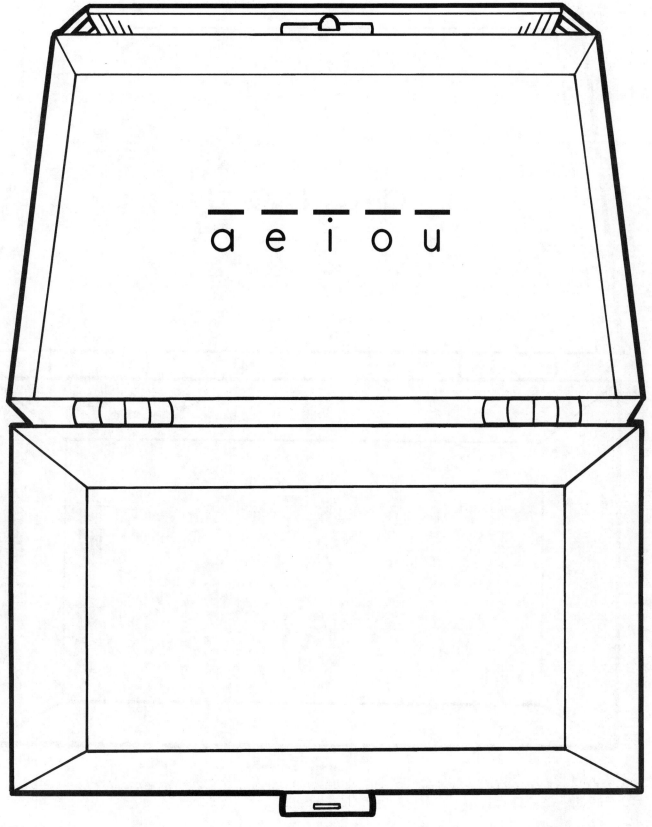

Lunch Break *(cont.)*

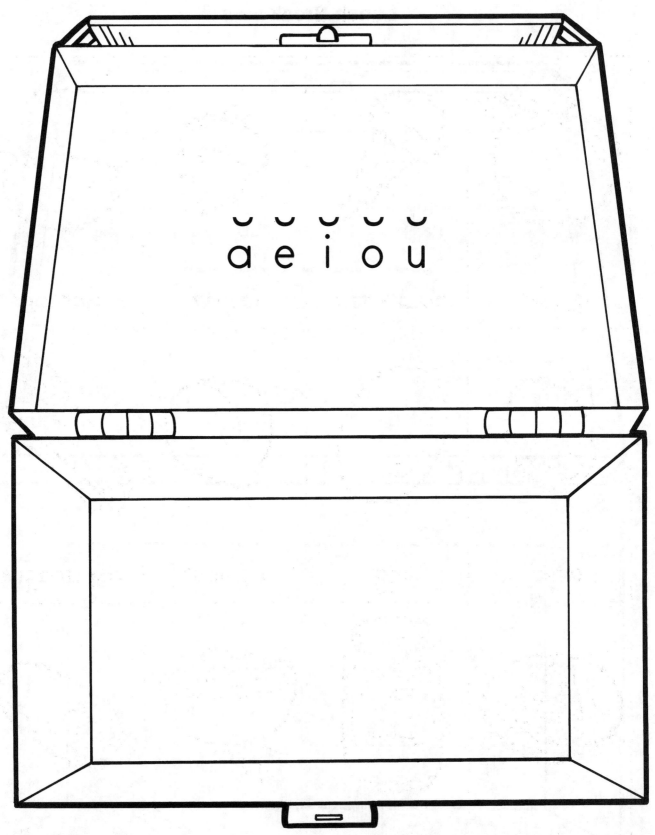

Lunch Break *(cont.)*

apple	ice cream	acorn	oatmeal
olive	egg	apricot	asparagus
enchilada	applesauce	escargot	egg roll

Number Blocks

Skill: Identifying Number Words

Materials: scissors; number cards/base (page 193); blocks (pages 194–195); helping page (page 196)

Teacher Preparation: Cut out numbers cards/base and blocks. Color and laminate number cards and blocks, if desired.

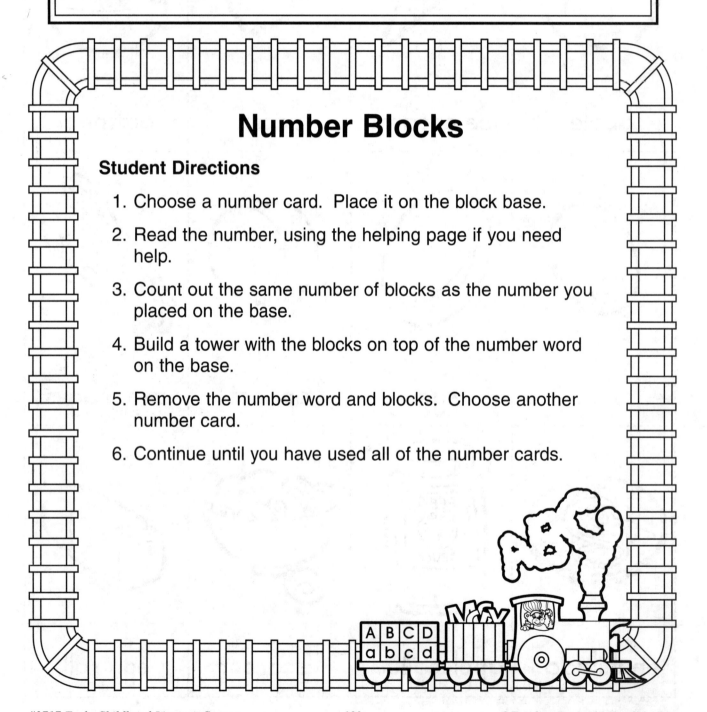

Number Blocks

Student Directions

1. Choose a number card. Place it on the block base.

2. Read the number, using the helping page if you need help.

3. Count out the same number of blocks as the number you placed on the base.

4. Build a tower with the blocks on top of the number word on the base.

5. Remove the number word and blocks. Choose another number card.

6. Continue until you have used all of the number cards.

Number Blocks *(cont.)*

one	two
three	four
five	six
seven	eight
nine	ten

Number Blocks *(cont.)*

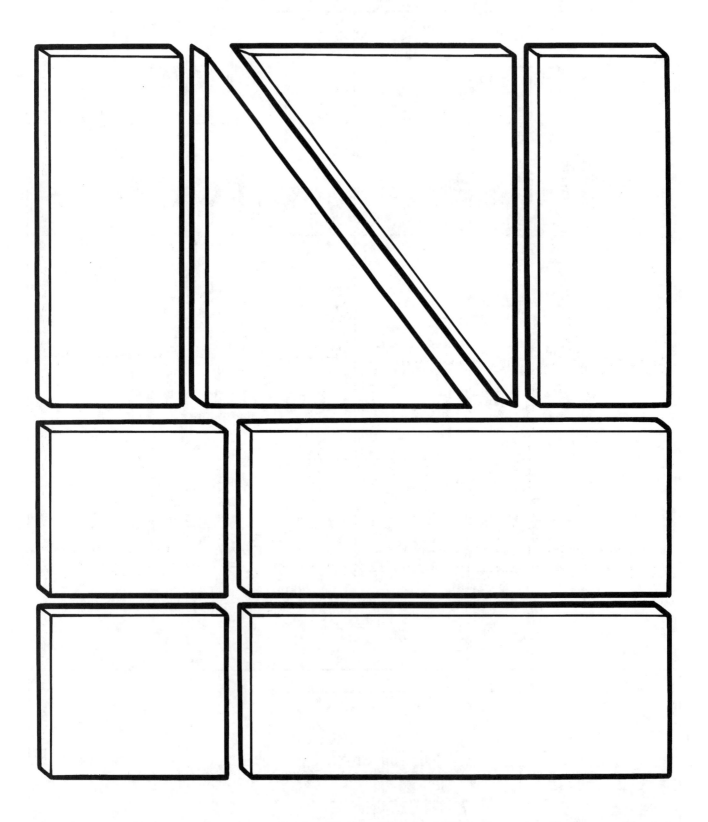

194

Number Blocks *(cont.)*

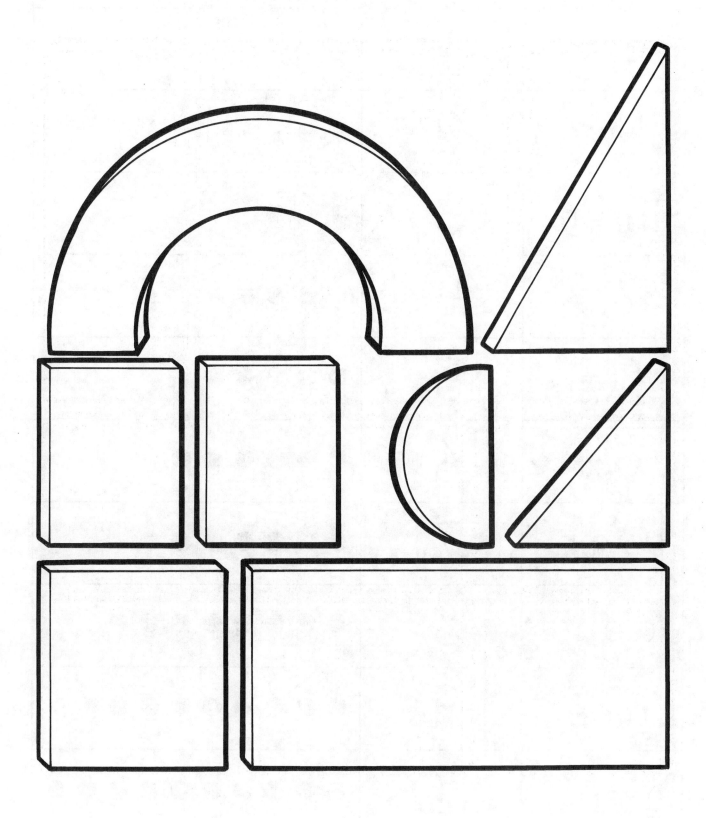

Number Blocks *(cont.)*
Helping Page

one	1	●
two	2	●●
three	3	●●●
four	4	●●●●
five	5	●●●●●
six	6	●●●●●●
seven	7	●●●●●●●
eight	8	●●●●●●●●
nine	9	●●●●●●●●●
ten	10	●●●●●●●●●●

Color Sort

Skill: Identifying Color Words

Materials: two copies of the crayon boxes (page 198); crayons (red, blue, yellow, green, purple, brown, orange, and black); scissors; crayons reproducible (pages 199–200); helping chart (page 201)

Teacher Preparation: Color each box a different color (one each, red, blue, yellow, green, purple, brown, orange and black.) Cut out crayons and crayon boxes. Laminate crayons and boxes, if desired. Color the helping chart crayons the indicated color.

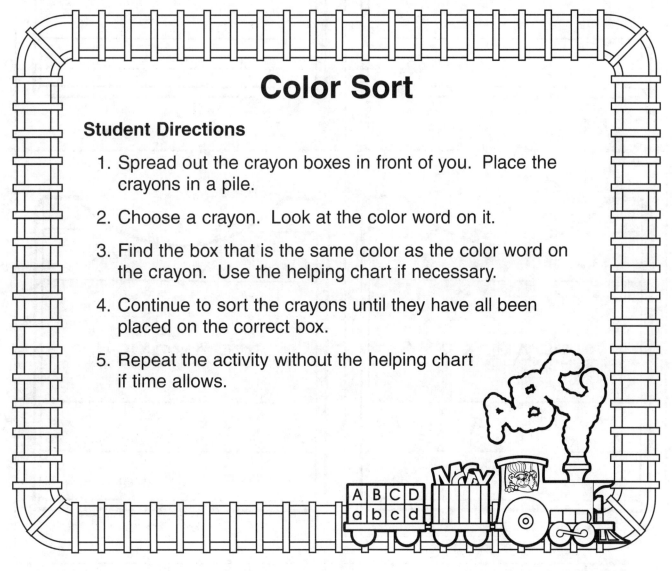

Color Sort

Student Directions

1. Spread out the crayon boxes in front of you. Place the crayons in a pile.

2. Choose a crayon. Look at the color word on it.

3. Find the box that is the same color as the color word on the crayon. Use the helping chart if necessary.

4. Continue to sort the crayons until they have all been placed on the correct box.

5. Repeat the activity without the helping chart if time allows.

Color Sort *(cont.)*

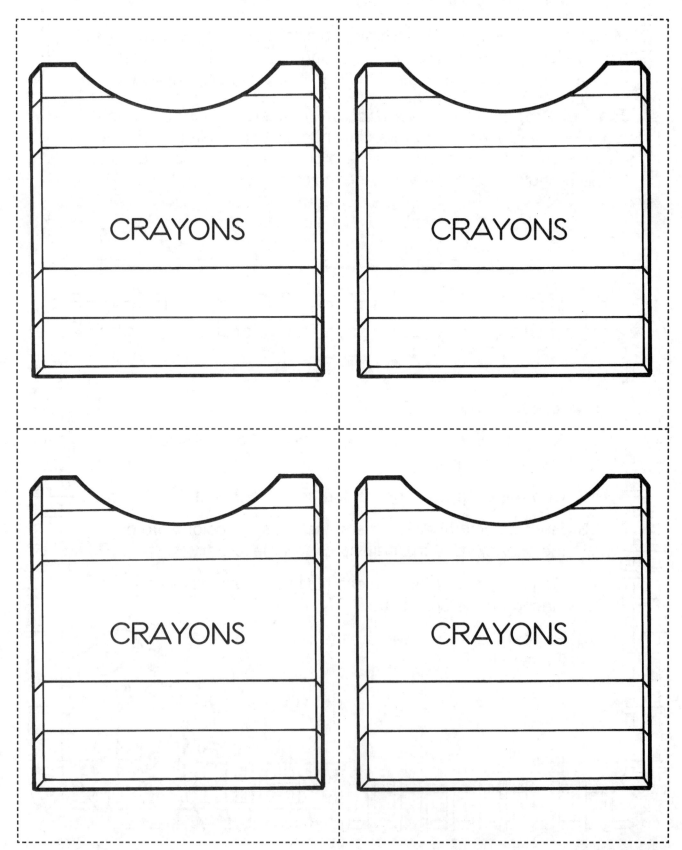

Color Sort *(cont.)*

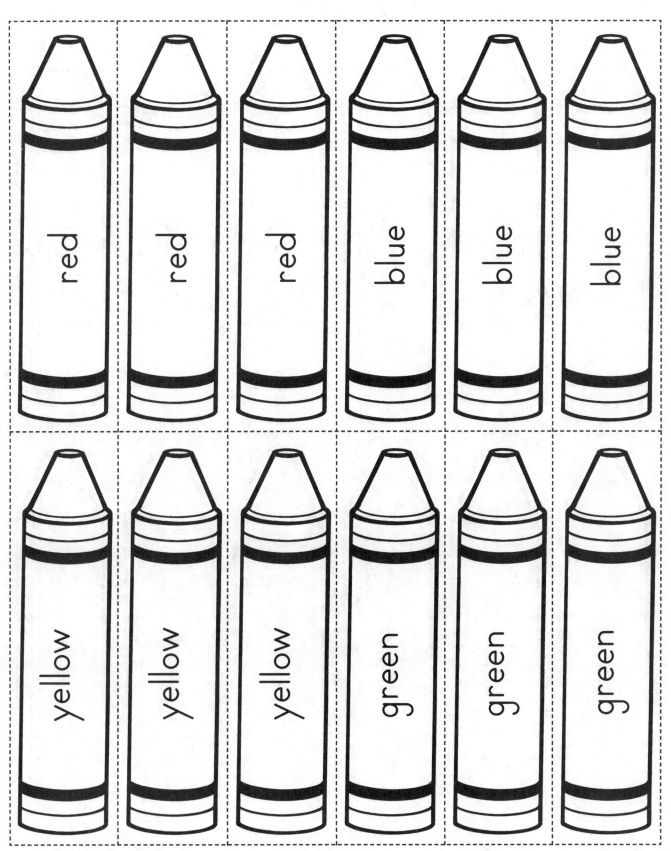

Color Sort *(cont.)*

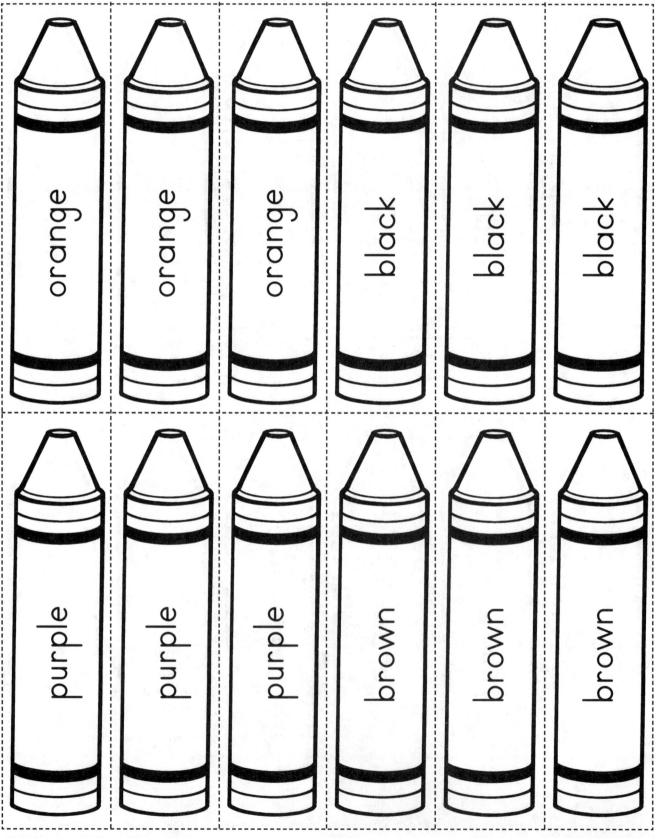

Color Sort *(cont.)*

Helping Chart Color Words

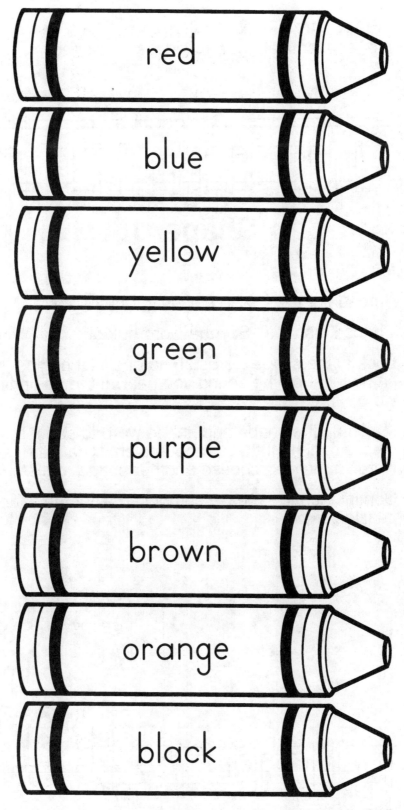

red

blue

yellow

green

purple

brown

orange

black

Shape Up!

Skill: Identifying Shape Words

Materials: scissors; shape word puzzles (pages 203–204)

Teacher Preparation: Cut out shape word puzzles on the dotted lines. Color and laminate puzzle pieces, if desired.

Shape Up!

Student Directions

1. Spread out the puzzle pieces in front of you.

2. Choose a shape. Say the word out loud.

3. Look at the shape words. Find one that begins with the same letter as the sound you hear at the beginning of the word.

4. Match up the shape and shape word to see if the puzzle pieces match. If they do not match, try another shape word. If they do, choose another shape to match.

5. Continue until you have completed all of the shape puzzles.

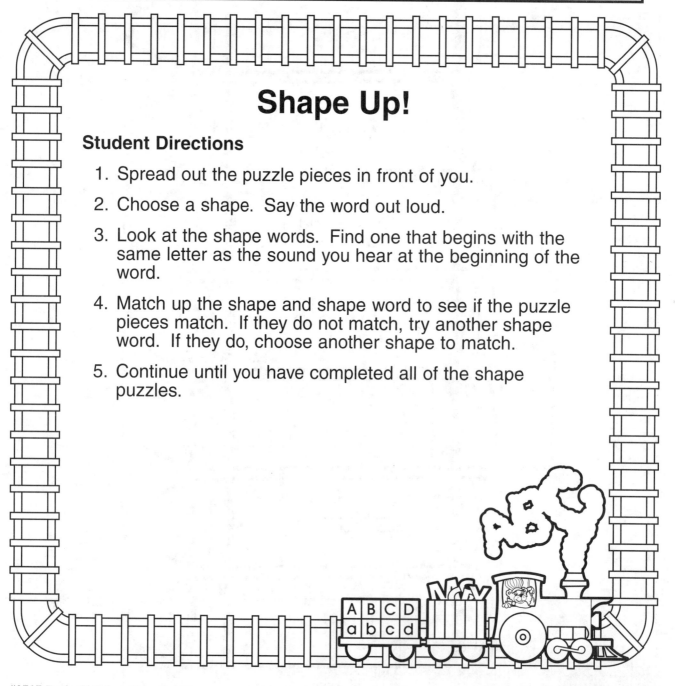

Shape Up! *(cont.)*

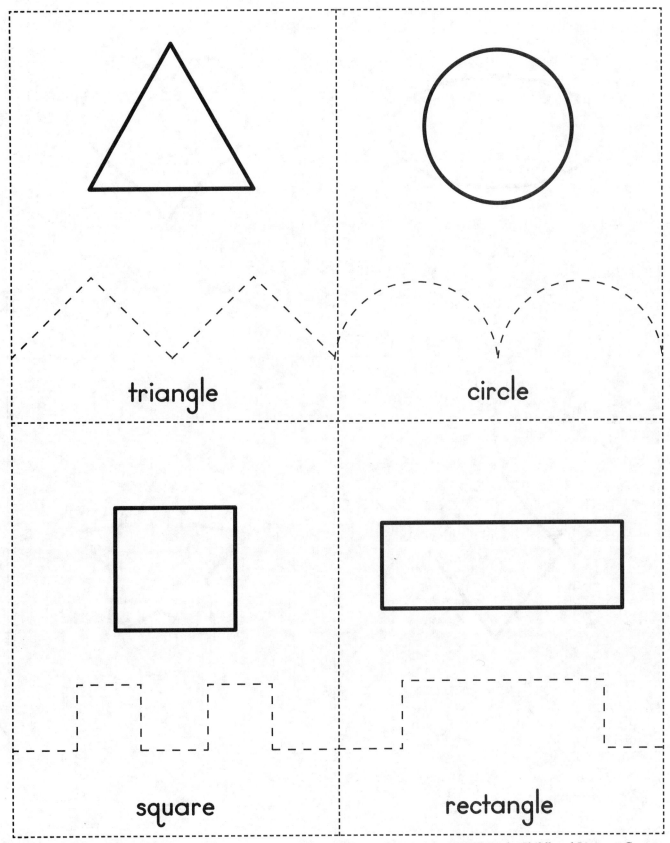

triangle

circle

square

rectangle

Shape Up! *(cont.)*

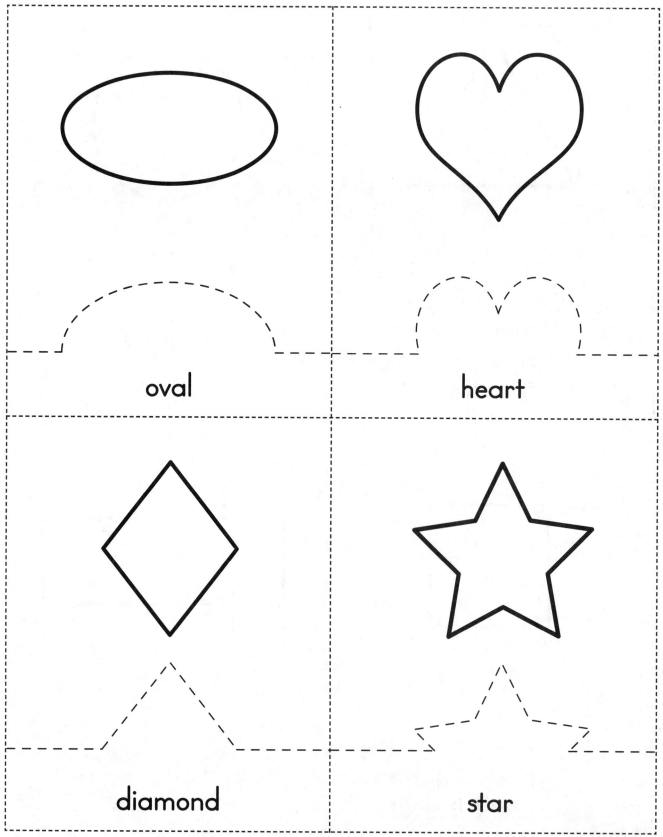

oval

heart

diamond

star

Sight Word Snowmen

Skill: Matching Basic Sight Words

Materials: scissors; snowmen (pages 206–208)

Teacher Preparation: Cut out snowmen. Color and laminate snowmen, if desired.

Sight Word Snowmen

Student Directions

1. Spread out the puzzle pieces in front of you.

2. Choose one snowman top and look at the word on it. Read it if you can.

3. Look for the snowman bottom with the matching word on it. Match the puzzle pieces. If the pieces do not match, try another bottom.

4. If the pieces match, find another top and look for its match.

5. Continue until all the sight words have been matched.

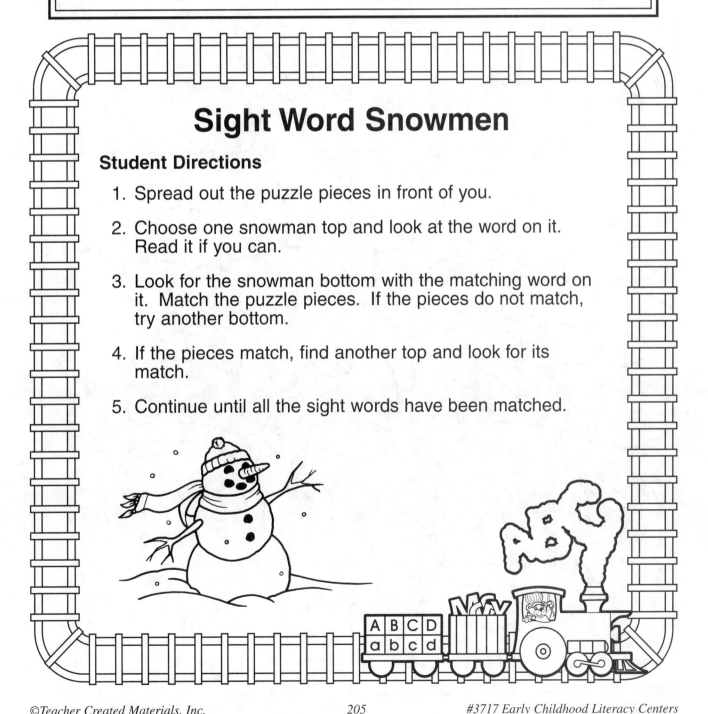

Sight Word Snowmen *(cont.)*

Sight Word Snowmen *(cont.)*

Sight Word Snowmen *(cont.)*

ABC

Skill: Identifying the Parts of a Book, Page Numbers; Alphabet Sequencing

Materials: student copies of book pages (pages 210–216); several children's books; scissors; student copies of the helping page (page 217); stapler; pencils

Teacher Preparation: Assemble the book pages for each student. Have a group discussion about books with your class. Talk about the components of a book (cover, title page, author and illustrator, and the page numbers). Display several books as examples. You may cutout the book pages or have the students do this.

ABC

Student Directions

1. Cut your mini-book pages on the dotted lines.
2. Spread out the pages out on the floor in front of you.
3. Find the cover with the large letters and a line for the author's name.
4. Look at the letters on each page and put the pages in order from A–Z. You can use the helping page if necessary.
5. When the pages are in the correct order, have your teacher help you staple them together.
6. Write your name on the cover. (You are the author of this book.)
7. Number the pages of the book by writing a different number in the circle at the bottom on each page. Look at the helping page if necessary.
8. Read the book to yourself or to a friend.

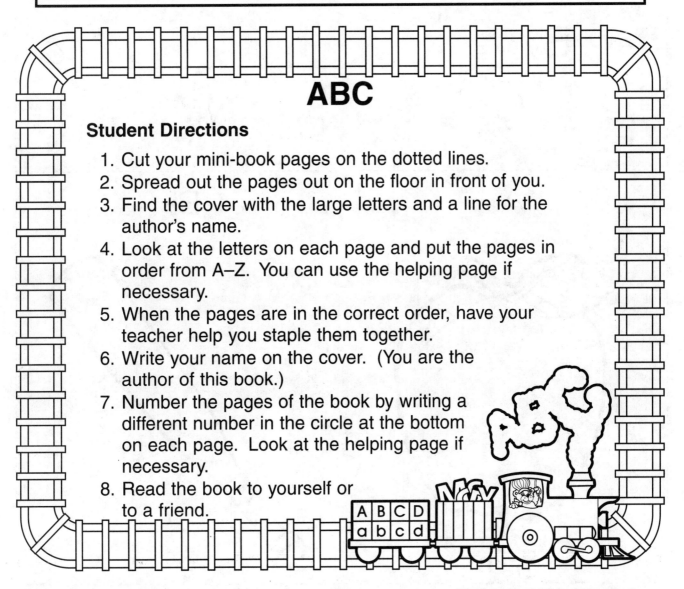

ABC *(cont.)*

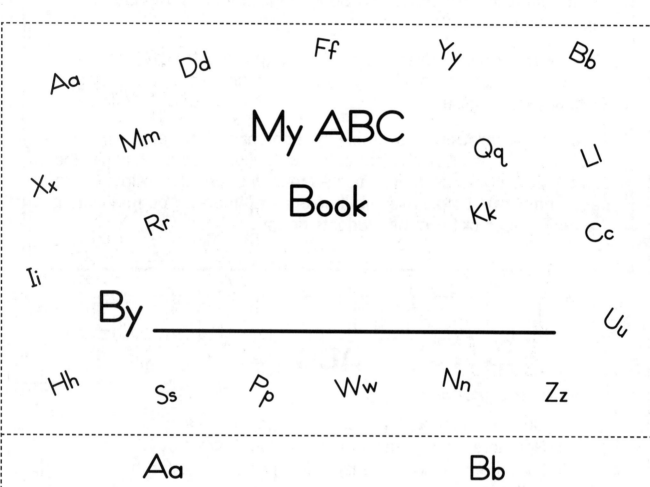

Aa Dd Ff Yy Bb

Mm Qq Ll

Xx Kk Cc

Rr

Ii Uu

My ABC

Book

By _____

Hh Ss Pp Ww Nn Zz

Aa

apple

Bb

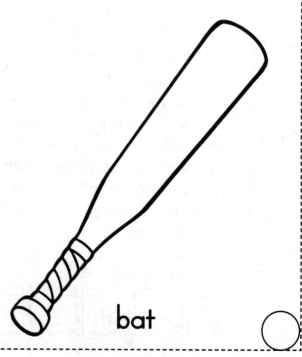

bat

ABC *(cont.)*

Cc

cat

Dd

dog

Ee

elephant

Ff

fan

ABC *(cont.)*

Gg

goat

Hh

heart

Ii

igloo

Jj

jar

ABC *(cont.)*

Kk

kite

Ll

lamp

Mm

monkey

Nn

nest

ABC *(cont.)*

Oo

octopus

Pp

pan

Qq

queen

Rr

rainbow

214

ABC *(cont.)*

Ss

snake

Tt

turtle

Uu

umbrella

Vv

van

ABC *(cont.)*

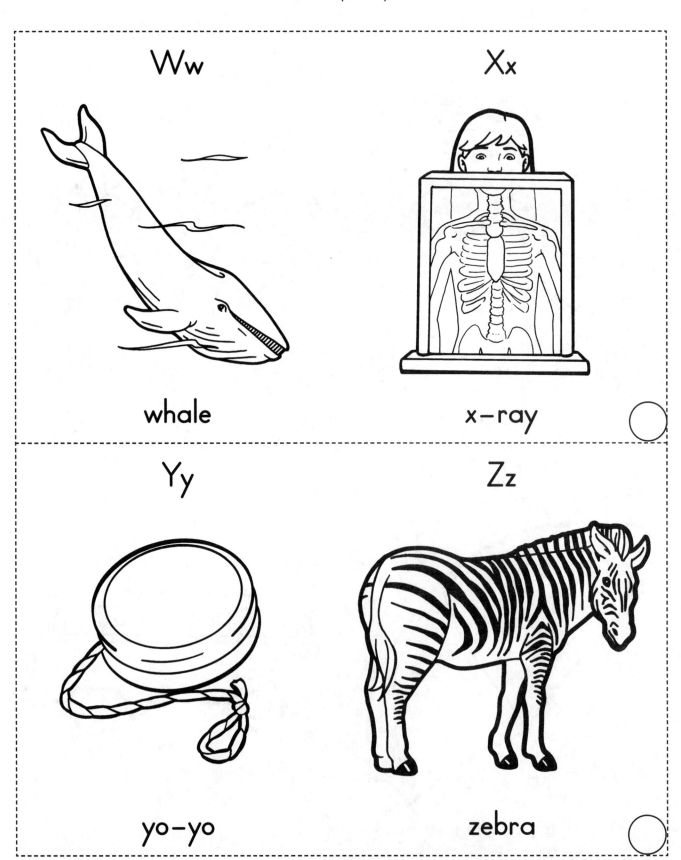

Ww

whale

Xx

x-ray

Yy

yo-yo

Zz

zebra

ABC *(cont.)*

ABC Mini Book
Helping Page

Aa Bb Cc Dd Ee Ff

Gg Hh Ii Jj Kk Ll

Mm Nn Oo Pp Qq Rr

Ss Tt Uu Vv Ww Xx

Yy Zz

1   2   3   4   5

6   7   8   9   10

11   12   13

Long and Short Vowels

Skill: Identifying Parts of a Book, Authors, and Illustrators

Materials: teacher copy of the book; student copies of book pages (page 219–221); student copies of the helping page (page 222); several children's books; scissors; stapler; pencils; crayons or markers

Teacher Preparation: Assemble the book pages for each student. Have a class discussion about authors and illustrators. Show the children several books and point out the name of the author and illustrator of each. You may want to find a Caldecott Award book and show the children the medal on the front of the book. Explain that the book has been given this award for its beautiful pictures, drawn by the illustrator. Show the children the long and short vowels mini-book. Explain that they will get to be the illustrator of their book.

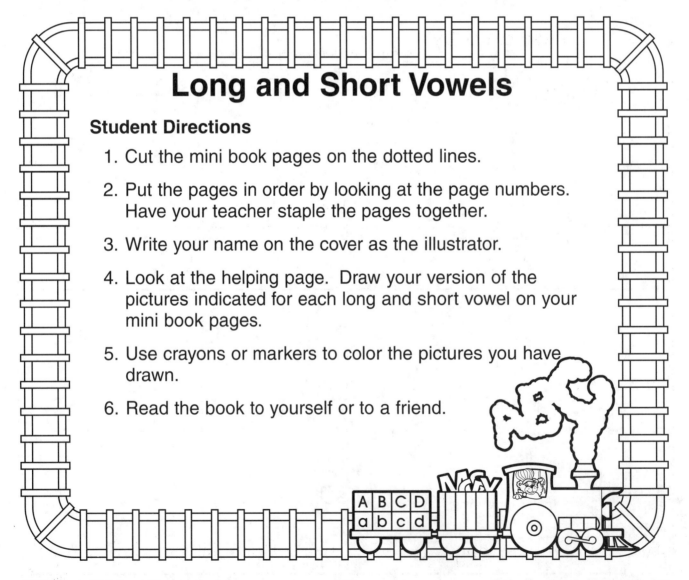

Long and Short Vowels

Student Directions

1. Cut the mini book pages on the dotted lines.

2. Put the pages in order by looking at the page numbers. Have your teacher staple the pages together.

3. Write your name on the cover as the illustrator.

4. Look at the helping page. Draw your version of the pictures indicated for each long and short vowel on your mini book pages.

5. Use crayons or markers to color the pictures you have drawn.

6. Read the book to yourself or to a friend.

Long and Short Vowels *(cont.)*

Uu Ee Ii

Aa Ee Oo

Ii Ee Uu

Long and Short Vowels

Oo

Ee Illustrated by _____

Oo Uu Oo Ii

Aa

Āā	Ăă
Acorn starts with long Aa.	Apple starts with short Aa.

(1)

Long and Short Vowels *(cont.)*

Ee

Ē ē

Eleven starts with long **Ee.**

Ĕ ĕ

Elephant starts with short **Ee.** ②

Ii

Ī ī

Ice cream starts with long **Ii.**

Ĭ ĭ

Igloo starts with short **Ii.** ③

Long and Short Vowels *(cont.)*

Oo

Ō ō

Ŏ ŏ

Oval starts with long Oo.

Octopus starts with short Oo. ④

Ii

Ū ū

Ŭ ŭ

Uniform starts with long Uu.

Umbrella starts with short Uu. ⑤

Long and Short Vowels *(cont.)*
Helping Page

Aa		Ee	
Āā	Ăă	Ēē	Ěě
acorn	apple	eleven	elephant

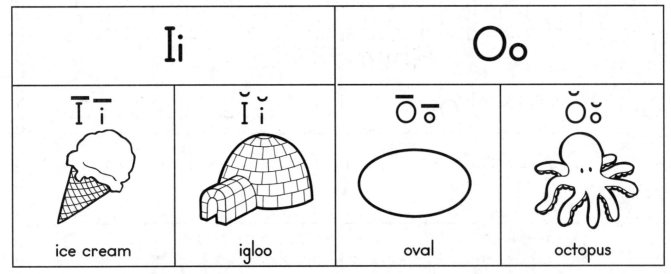

Ii		Oo	
Īī	Ĭĭ	Ōō	Ŏŏ
ice cream	igloo	oval	octopus

Uu	
Ūū	Ŭŭ
uniform	umbrella

Rhyme Time

Skill: Identifying the Parts of a Book, Left to Right and Top to Bottom Text, Identifying Rhyming Words

Materials: student copies of book pages (pages 224–227); student copies of picture cards (page 228); stapler; a children's big book; pencils; glue; crayons or markers

Teacher Preparation: Assemble a mini book for each student by putting the pages in order and stapling them together on the left side. Have a class discussion about the text of a book. Explain to the class that text in our language goes from top to bottom and left to right. Read a Big Book to the class and trace your finger under the words to illustrate your point. Show the class the Rhyme Time mini-book and explain that they will help complete the text in their books.

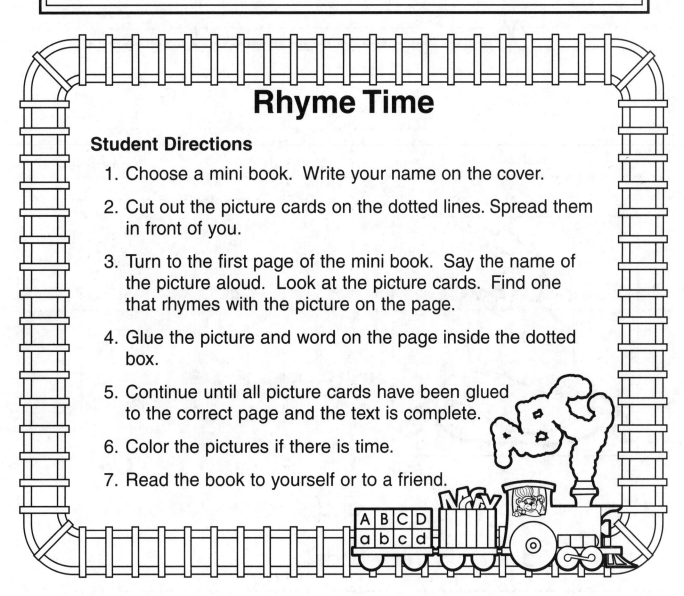

Rhyme Time

Student Directions

1. Choose a mini book. Write your name on the cover.

2. Cut out the picture cards on the dotted lines. Spread them in front of you.

3. Turn to the first page of the mini book. Say the name of the picture aloud. Look at the picture cards. Find one that rhymes with the picture on the page.

4. Glue the picture and word on the page inside the dotted box.

5. Continue until all picture cards have been glued to the correct page and the text is complete.

6. Color the pictures if there is time.

7. Read the book to yourself or to a friend.

Rhyme Time *(cont.)*

Rhyme Time

By _____

Cat   and

are rhyming words.

⓵

Rhyme Time *(cont.)*

Wig   and

are rhyming words.

②

Dog   and

are rhyming words.

③

Rhyme Time *(cont.)*

Fox   and

are rhyming words.

4

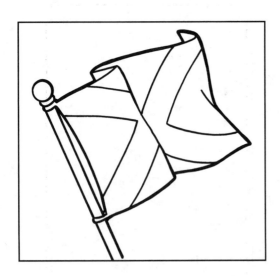

Flag   and

are rhyming words.

5

Rhyme Time *(cont.)*

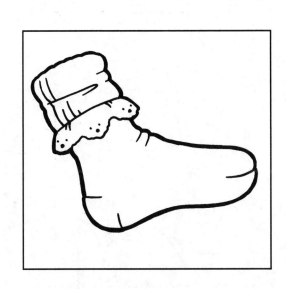

Sock   and

are rhyming words.

⑥

Jar   and

are rhyming words.

⑦

Rhyme Time *(cont.)*

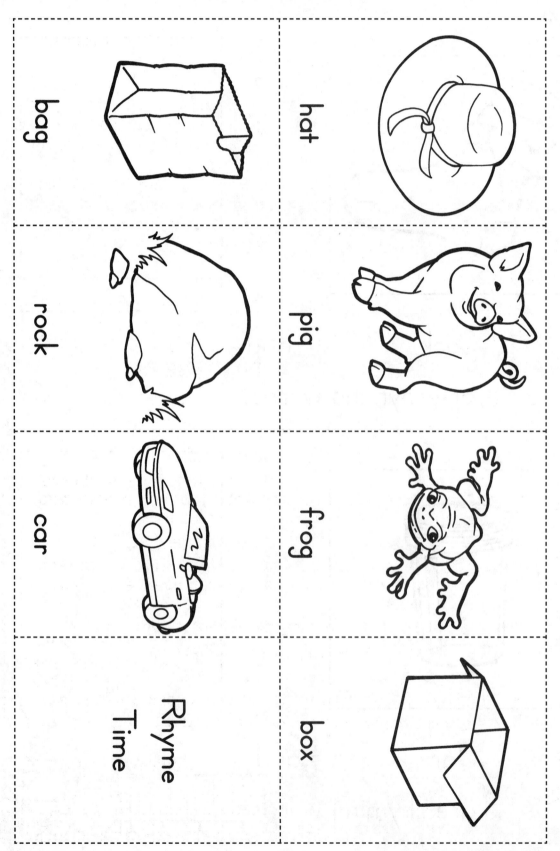

bag

hat

rock

pig

car

frog

Rhyme Time

box

Colors and Numbers

Skill: Identifying Parts of a Book, Text; Recognizing Color and Number Words

Materials: student copies of book pages (pages 230–235); scissors; stapler; student copies of word cards (page 236); crayons; several children's books; pencils; glue; helping page (235)

Teacher Preparation: Assemble the book pages for each student. (The helping page will be used as the last page of the book.) Reproduce word cards for each student. Help students color in the crayons on the helping page before they begin the center. Have a class discussion about the words in the books. Explain that the words in a book are called the text and the text is what gives the book meaning. Show several examples of books with text. Show the class the Colors and Numbers mini-book and explain that they will get to add text to their books.

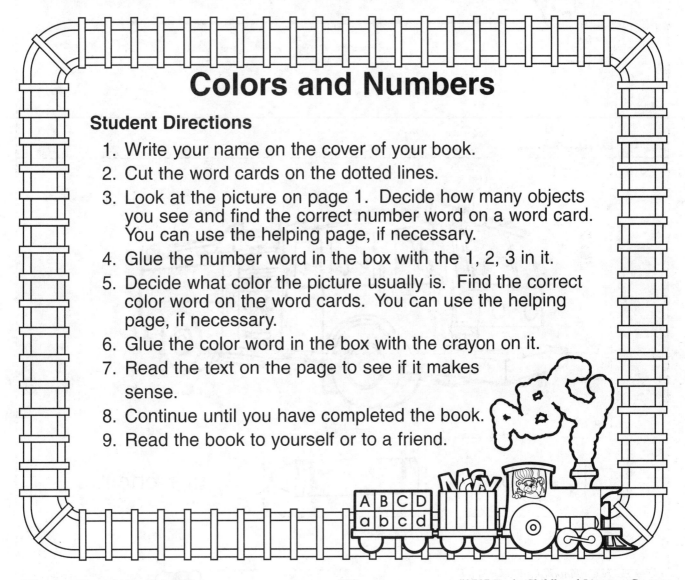

Colors and Numbers

Student Directions

1. Write your name on the cover of your book.

2. Cut the word cards on the dotted lines.

3. Look at the picture on page 1. Decide how many objects you see and find the correct number word on a word card. You can use the helping page, if necessary.

4. Glue the number word in the box with the 1, 2, 3 in it.

5. Decide what color the picture usually is. Find the correct color word on the word cards. You can use the helping page, if necessary.

6. Glue the color word in the box with the crayon on it.

7. Read the text on the page to see if it makes sense.

8. Continue until you have completed the book.

9. Read the book to yourself or to a friend.

Colors and Numbers *(cont.)*

Colors and Numbers

By _____

| 1, 2, 3 |  | fire engine. |

(1)

Colors and Numbers *(cont.)*

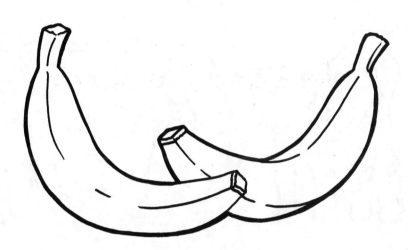

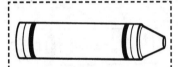 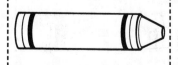 bananas.

②

1, 2, 3 frogs.

③

Colors and Numbers *(cont.)*

1, 2, 3      elephants.

④

1, 2, 3   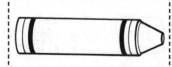   pigs.

⑤

Colors and Numbers *(cont.)*

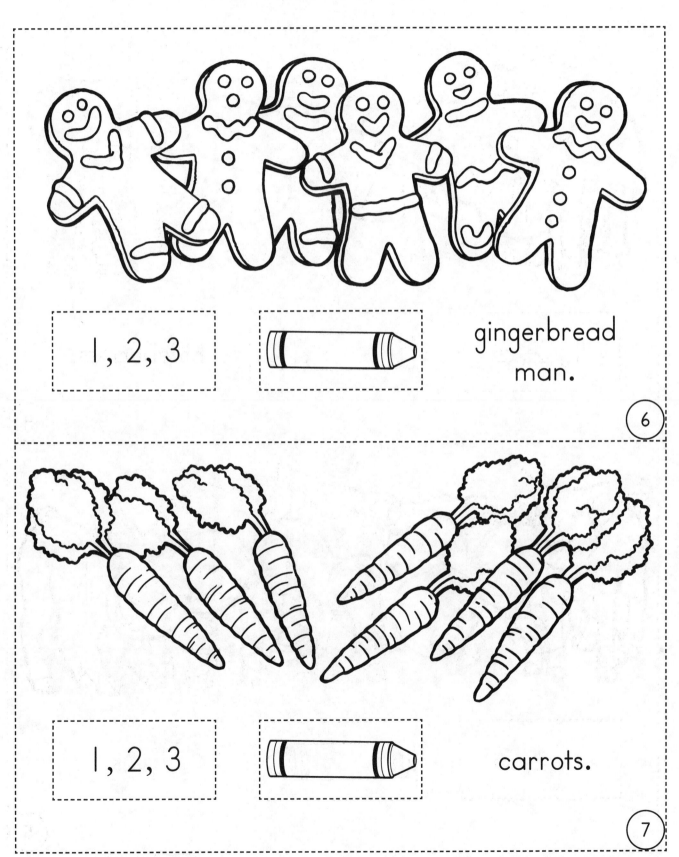

1, 2, 3   gingerbread man.

6

1, 2, 3   carrots.

7

Colors and Numbers *(cont.)*

1, 2, 3 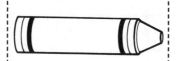 blueberries.

⑧

1, 2, 3 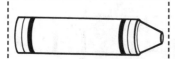 olives.

⑨

Colors and Numbers *(cont.)*

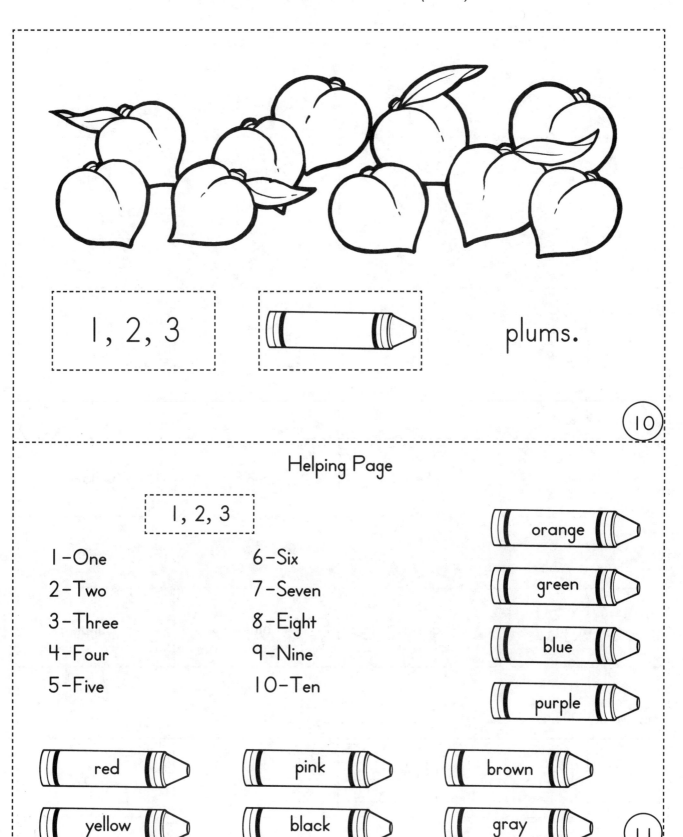

1, 2, 3   [crayon]   plums.

⑩

Helping Page

1, 2, 3

1–One	6–Six
2–Two	7–Seven
3–Three	8–Eight
4–Four	9–Nine
5–Five	10–Ten

orange

green

blue

purple

red

pink

brown

yellow

black

gray

⑪

Colors and Numbers *(cont.)*

One	Two	Three	Four

Five	Six	Seven	Eight

Nine	Ten	red	yellow

orange	green	blue	purple

pink	black	brown	gray

Alphabet

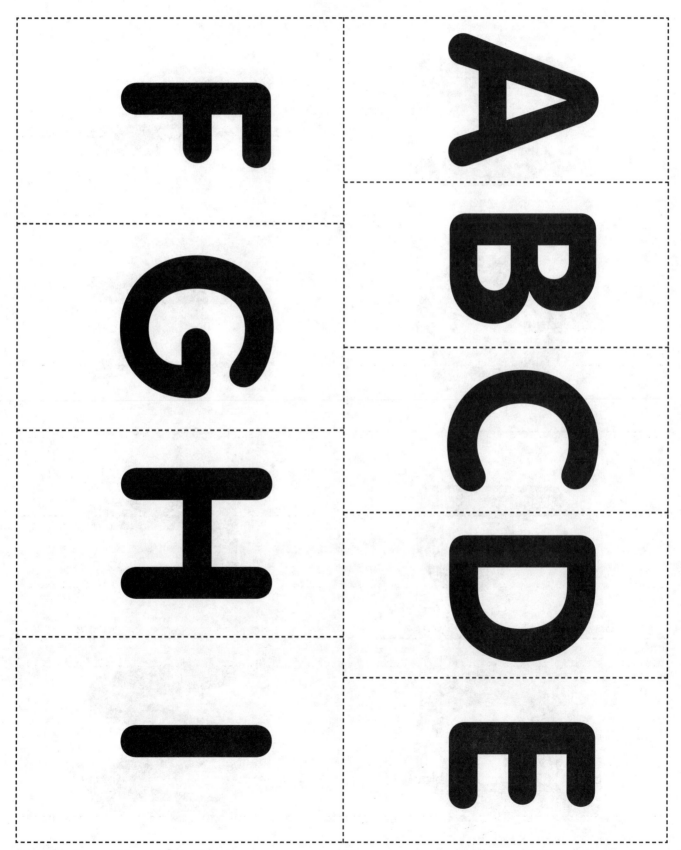

Alphabet *(cont.)*

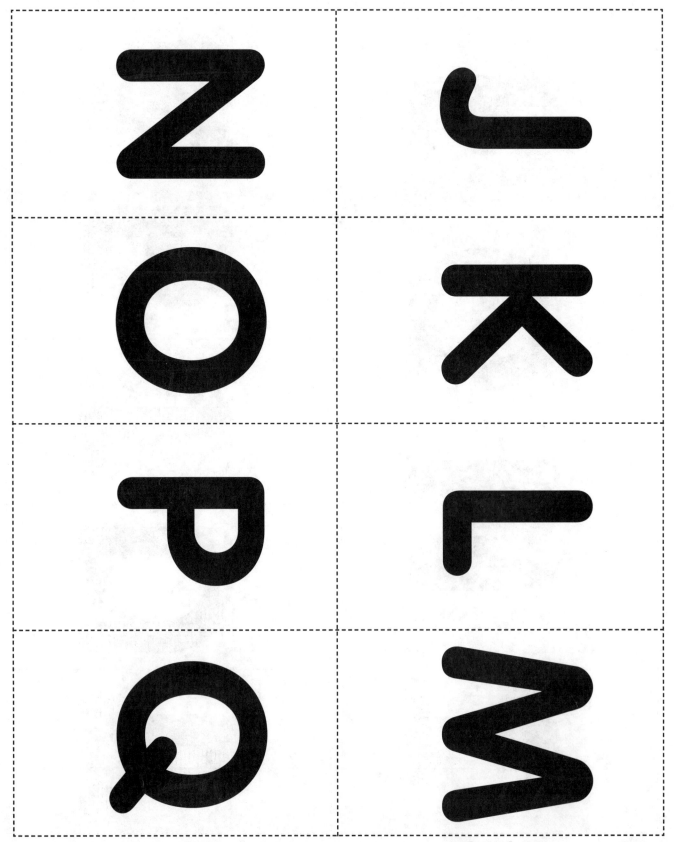

Alphabet *(cont.)*

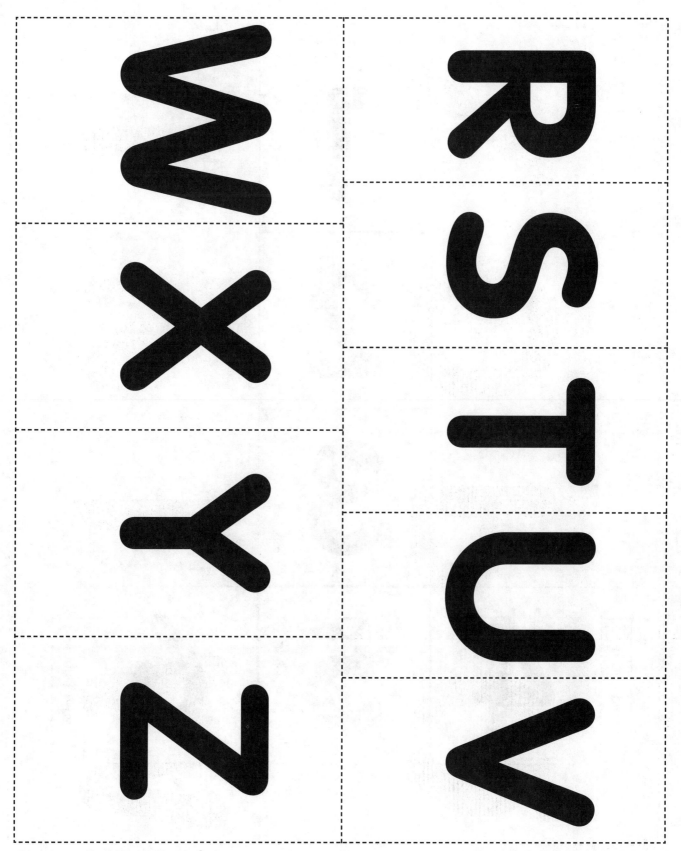

Number Cube